*A*dversity
*B*uilds
*C*haracter

AN INSPIRATIONAL TRUE LIFE STORY
OF DISABILITY, ADDICTION AND ACCEPTANCE

By
Tom Ufert

iUniverse, Inc.
Bloomington

Adversity Builds Character
An Inspirational True Life Story of Disability, Addiction and Acceptance

iUniverse books may be ordered through booksellers or by contacting:

iUniverse
1663 Liberty Drive
Bloomington, IN 47403
www.iuniverse.com
1-800-Authors (1-800-288-4677)

ISBN: 978-1-4759-5271-1 (sc)
ISBN: 978-1-4759-5273-5 (hc)
ISBN: 978-1-4759-5272-8 (e)

Library of Congress Control Number: 2012918006

Printed in the United States of America

iUniverse rev. date: 10/2/2012

Contents

Dedication

This account of my life is dedicated with love and admiration to the two human beings most responsible for the man I have become. Each in their own way did the best they knew how and never stopped loving me for the person I was. They loved all that I was, all that I am, and all that I possess of becoming.

To my mother, Gloria Edith Riley Ufert, I dedicate this book for she made the greatest sacrifice a mother can make — her own child. Her deep love for me overcame every other human emotion, seeking only the best possible future for me, her son.

I dedicate this book to my godmother/grandmother, Joy Vickery Campbell, for she gave the greatest gift an unrelated human being can make — unconditional love. Her guidance, integrity, support and faith sustained me through all times good and bad. Her inspiration was the driving force behind this book and my life, giving meaning to both.

Their gifts to me of life and love made my life story possible. I pray their inspirational love may give others the hope and strength to overcome their adversities.

Preface

Over the last several years many friends and acquaintances have suggested that I should write a book. Though I have considered my experiences to be merely the regular trials and tribulations of everyday life, many people insisted that my outlook and positive attitude could truly help and inspire others dealing with rough times. It is my sincerest hope that this book might indeed help in some small way.

My views and opinions are the result of experiences and encounters that I have been blessed with through my short life. I have said many times that if it were within my power to change a single moment in my life, I would not do so. Every single micro-second of my life has made me the man I am today, *and of that I am proud*. Like all human beings there are things I have said or done that I am not proud of. However, in hindsight they have made me who I am today. Without them my life would be incomplete. Sharon Duhon Smith, my high school senior English teacher, had a poster that still lives with me today: "We only fail when we fail to try!" There are no failures or mistakes in life unless we fail to learn from them. I can only hope that the lessons I have learned may be of help to others: the intended beneficiaries of my thoughts.

It must be noted here that everything I have written is from my own interpretation; others that may have been present or privy to additional facts might see things differently. That is okay, this is my story not theirs. I only pray that my version is close to the actual truth and that it doesn't harm anyone in the process. *I believe there are always at least three sides to every story: yours, mine, and the truth: sometimes two of these are the same.* Regardless of personal opinions, my sole intention in writing

Adversity Builds Character is to help other people as others have helped me. By the grace of God, I hope that I succeed.

You have already read my dedication but now I must also make a few acknowledgements. I owe the title, among other things, to Joy Campbell (my Godmother/Grandmother). She stressed for many years that "adversity builds character," and she was so right. I would not be half the person I am today were it not for the adversities I have endured. Therein also lays my deepest gratitude to God Himself; without knowing suffering in life, how could I possibly appreciate the magnificent awe and wonder of all creation or of my fellow man. That, I believe, is the true lesson of Christ's life.

In addition I owe endless gratitude to my "adopted" parents Chuck and Karen Campbell. My original subtitle, *A SECOND CHANCE*, partly reflected the awesome gift they bestowed by offering me a "second chance" at life. I have learned however, life itself is full of "second chances" if one is gifted with the insight to recognize them. My life story is full of them! Before Chuck and Karen took me into their home my path was certainly clouded and troublesome. Not only did they provide a good stable home of love and structure, but they nurtured an appreciation for education and some of the finer things life has to offer — a gift I can never repay. They are the type of people who do not require recognition for their efforts; rather the satisfaction of achievement alone will suffice. My love for them can never be surpassed, though time, circumstance, and geography may separate us.

There are an endless number of truly magnificent people I have had the great honor of knowing and sharing but brief moments in time with. There are far too many for me to name here, but I will make every effort throughout my tale to give them the love and credit they so rightly deserve. Over time I have decided to alter some names and details of events for the dignity and discretion of those still living. For those individuals they will surely recognize my recollections and know in their hearts the truth of what I write; I can only hope and pray they fully understand "the method to my madness." Regardless, to each of them I say, thank God for being in my life!

Then one of them, when he saw that he was healed, turned back, praising God with a loud voice then prostrated himself at Jesus' feet and thanked Him. And he was a Samaritan.
Then Jesus asked, "Were not ten made clean? But the other nine, where are they? Was none of them found to return and give praise to God except this foreigner?"
Then He said to him, "Get up and go on your way; your faith has made you well."

Luke 17: 13-19

I wanted to write this book for a number of reasons, but none could compare with the unquenchable need to shout to all creation the praises of God; not just for being alive but perhaps more importantly for being more human. In that one defining phrase I discovered what I think we all strive to comprehend — only in being more human do we "get it!" When we accept who we are, for all our faults and graces, only then do we begin to understand our true nature and therein our relationship to each other, all creation, and God Himself. How can we possibly be close to God and our fellow men if we are trying so hard to conquer both?

I remember as a small boy, don't ask me when or where, but that the "old" people were talking over coffee. Children were supposed to be outside playing or inside sitting quietly (no small task for a brat such as yours truly). It was just such a setting and one of those rare occasions when I was tame enough to be regarded as a human child, that I must have heard *ABC* for the first time. If my memory serves correctly, the subject involved the unfortunate fate of a family friend troubled by ill health. I distinctly remember Grandma Campbell saying "*Adversity*

Builds Character" and implying that some good would inevitably come from the hardship. Unfamiliar with the word adversity, and I guess wanting to obtain some of the room's captivated attention for myself; I asked what the word meant. Past experience should have foretold the obvious reply; "Thomas if you don't know what a word means, go look it up in the dictionary." For some reason, of all the similar childhood experiences I had, this one has stood out. It wasn't until some twenty years later that I penned "*Adversity Builds Character*" into my title.

For me "*ABC*" is a multifaceted concept and one that I hope can help other people deal with the struggles of everyday life. The ideas are so powerful and yet so simplistic that like sub-atomic particles, they can be lost from sight all too easily. From the moment of conception the body begins to die and the spirit begins to whither. Yet preoccupation with that fact is one of the most driving impulses in the human psyche. We spend our whole lives trying to put off the undeniable and inevitable conclusion of our existence as we know it. Yet knowing our life clock is ticking doesn't seem to empower us to utilize that which we have. *Adversity Builds Character* was written with three major ideas in mind; first, life *is* a bed of roses, *but not without thorns*. Second, no matter how bad your life is, just take a look around and *you'll find someone who has it worse*. Finally, like the poem "Footsteps in the Sand" God is always with you and He never gives you more than you can *really* handle. For me all of this comes full circle in Robert Frost's poem "The Road Less Taken,"

> *Somewhere ages and ages hence I shall be telling this,*
> *Two roads diverged in a wood, and I,*
> *I took the one less traveled by,*
> *And that has made all the difference.*

I am NOT perfect!!! Nor does this book seek to diminish the reader's own trials and tribulations. Rather it was written to help espouse the mental breakthrough that while *unique* in every detail, we are commonly linked to each other and therein lay the key to our future. Only when a man can set aside his own selfish, almost animalistic desires for self-preservation in the wake of another's needs, does he find that divine essence in humanity and himself. For only then can we see that forgiveness is divine and since we are all sinners, a purely human condition, we come closest to God when we accept our true humanity for all that it is.

I sought, in writing this book, to use my life experiences, good and bad, to help others. So often through my life people have said how tough I've had it. Yet upon reflection it's been a wonderful life and if I could go back to change any millisecond of it, *I would not!* Everything that has happened has made me the man I am today, and of that fact, I am proud. *Life is as life is — either accept it or change it!* I only need to reflect upon the poor souls who have suffered through Rwanda, Yugoslavia, Krakow, the Sudan, 9/11, Katrina, Fukoshima, the Sandusky scandal, etc... to fully appreciate how blessed I am. I have food in my gut, a roof over my head, clothes on my back, a little money to get by on, friends who care about me, and those who love me - *REALLY, WHAT ELSE MATTERS?* It gives one pause when we want to whine and complain about how bad our lives are!

1

CRASH!

WHEN I OPENED my eyes all I could see was light. Lying flat on my back my vision and my mind were all a haze. Slowly out of the corner of my eye I saw movement and it was Brandon. He approached my bed with a tear streaked face that was as white as a ghost. I knew something was wrong but vaguely just assumed it was the pain medication I had been given following the previous night's car accident. At that very moment I still had no idea as to the extent of my injuries. Brandon seemed confused if not dumbfounded that I was clueless of my condition. He asked "don't you realize why you are lying flat on your back or that 20 pounds of weighted tongs are attached to your head?" Then it hit me and the memories started flooding my mind like a tidal wave.

The date was September 28, 1992. The time was around 3:30 on that Saturday morning as I struggled to climb into my silver blue Honda Civic. Suddenly Bobby Beth, one of my pool playing buddies from the bar, drove up in a bright red sports car. Though Bobby's demeanor and reputation gave me reason to doubt his character, I was blinded by a frustrated libido and the hope of a quick fix. Through the open window he asked where I was heading. I halfheartedly explained that it was late and I was on my way home before my lover got off work. He suggested we take a short joyride so that I could "experience the thrill of 'his' sports car." Though he appeared sober enough, I had easily observed his steady beer guzzling throughout the night and should have known better. We started out at a smooth normal pace. But then we hit the highway. Before I knew it Bobby was racing the Mazda RX seven at 80 miles an hour. Just as I voiced my deep concern that he was driving too fast, Bobby suddenly turned off the interstate onto a high climbing ramp leading back into downtown Dallas. Fearing arrest or an accident I was anxious to return to my parked car and head home. The next moment would change my life forever.

Halfway up the ramp, speeding at near 80 miles an hour, the driver's side of the car suddenly scraped the guard rail. In a split second Bobby lost control of the vehicle as we spiraled in a 180° fashion that slammed the vehicle fiercely against the guardrail causing it to tumble over twice before landing to a sudden stop. I must have passed out briefly because my next memory was that of a female African American police officer shining a flashlight into my eyes. I vaguely remember her asking my name and age before telling me not to move, that help was on the way. I do not remember anything after that until I was being rolled into Parkland Hospital's emergency room on a stretcher. A nurse, walking rapidly beside me, was rambling off a series of questions and statements. I do remember telling her not to call my roommate, Brandon, until midday the next day because he was working the late shift as an agency nurse and needed his sleep.

The next day around noon was when I opened my eyes to see the bright light and Brandon approaching. I had been diagnosed with multiple sclerosis only the month before. Now I was informed of an incomplete spinal fracture to the fifth and sixth cervical vertebrae in my neck. All the doctors' statements of diagnosis and prognosis were sketchy. Only time would tell to what degree I would recover from this near fatal injury. After two days in ICU with the weighted tongs dangling downward from my forehead, I was transferred to a private room for 24 hour observation. The 20 pound weighted tongs had been replaced with a 27 pound titanium metal halo literally screwed into my skull. Its purpose was to prevent my head and neck from moving in the hopes that my incomplete spinal fracture would heal naturally so as to avoid the need for a surgical cure. This extremely heavy and cumbersome metal "cage" was comprised of a thick metal ring clasped around the top of my head and was supported by four 18 inch metal rods that were attached to shoulder braces. The halo's additional weight totally wrecked any sense of orientation and equilibrium. In addition to this hardware, my spinal injury had resulted in significant swelling of the spinal cord itself causing extreme paralysis to three of my four limbs. With extreme effort and fatigue I was able to partially facilitate trunk movement of my upper torso, but had no sensory perception or neuromuscular control of my lower body. In essence it initially appeared that I was paralyzed from the waist down. Naturally this also required routine use of a catheter to perform normal urinary functions. As far as renal capabilities I was at the mercy of my bodily functions and required constant assistance from medical personnel to clean up my feces.

Any prognosis of complete or even partial recovery was bleak at best. Vaguely, I recall the intense discussion between Brandon, myself, and the attending specialist regarding future plans for my lengthy physical rehabilitation. The specialist stressed vigorously the merits of sending me to Baylor Rehabilitation Hospital noting its reputation as the most qualified facility for the type of medical care I would require. However, Brandon was strongly in favor of relocating me to the Plano rehab hospital where he had been serving on staff for the last several months. Admitting that Plano was significantly smaller and more accustomed to elderly patients recovering from hip and knee replacement surgery, Brandon relayed that he had already been in communication with the pertinent authorities; they had expressed confidence in their ability to properly fulfill my recuperation needs. Furthermore, he stressed the positive benefits of being able to daily monitor my progress while performing his duties at work. Privately, he conveyed that the strain of working all day at one facility and having to drive daily across town to another would be unbearable. Therefore, it was decided I would be transferred to Plano.

As a side note, Bobby Beth made a very brief visit to my room prior to my transfer. Lasting barely three minutes he made some cordial inquiries as to my condition and then offered a halfhearted token apology for the accident. In my heavily medicated state it was quite difficult to ascertain his genuine sincerity or true intent. However, in time he would reveal his true colors! I would never see him again.

Plano Rehabilitation Hospital (PRH) was a private two story 48 bed facility originally designed to care for the rehabilitative needs of the affluent Plano community's elderly. It had an excellent reputation for such care but I would be their first spinal cord patient, and certainly their youngest. The hospital's patient care model was organized around a therapeutic team design. Every aspect of the patient's rehabilitative care was structured around a therapy team of physical therapists, occupational therapists, speech therapists, respiratory therapists, recreational therapists, dietitians, nurses, social workers, and of course neurosurgeons. The patient's own team met weekly to discuss and review their therapy progress. My particular case presented these rehab experts with a new set of challenges, but they were eager and felt completely confident of our mutual success.

From the beginning, there was a special dedicated interest in my rehabilitation because of the connection the staff had with their friend and coworker, my roommate and lover of two years, Brandon. As well, my admission into PRH carried another significantly unique distinction: I was the only patient to have a room all to myself. It would be well over a month before the significance of this factor would become evident. This singular condition would be the third adversity to strike

4

at my very core in 1992, and it would nearly be the one that broke me. It had completely escaped my attention for the first few weeks of my rehab therapy that attached to the door of my hospital room was a bright red warning of biohazard. On one particular afternoon after returning from a very exhausting session of physical therapy I inquired from my personal nurse, Phil, as to the reason for this notification. Innocently and obviously unaware of my ignorance, he simply remarked it was because of my condition. The confused look upon my face and my insistence that I had no idea as to what he was referring caused an immediate facial expression of shock and alarm. He proceeded to explain that hospital regulations required a public warning because of my HIV positive status. My response was immediate. Physically, either from exhaustion or psychological shock, my body totally collapsed. Within minutes Dr. R was summoned accompanied by Brandon to explain that tests of my blood chemistry from my emergency room admission had indicated the presence of the HIV virus. I was completely blown away! Either as a result of my injuries or significant pain medication, my recollection of this diagnosis having been conveyed to me before now, was nonexistent. The emotional and psychological effects of this news were devastating. For the next several days I was completely incapacitated due to extreme depression. Members of the staff naturally understood. In fact they had only questioned *when, not if,* my positive mental attitude would be shaken by the realization and acceptance of this "death sentence."

What broke my debilitating state of depression, I cannot explain. All I know is that one morning I awoke and my entire mental attitude and approach to life had completely changed. My only explanation is the grace of God and divine intervention. From that moment on, overcoming my adversities and the sheer will to live were the driving forces that compelled me to survive. My future was uncertain. Undoubtedly, the road ahead would be long and hard. Remembering the painful and arduous struggle my mom had endured for ten long years drove me to never giving in. All of the support and encouragement of Brandon, my coworkers at Sister's Insurance Company, and especially the hard working medical staff at PRH spurned me on to overcome these trials and tribulations. Even more importantly the regular visits from Eucharistic ministers at the local Catholic Church reaffirmed my faith in God proving that regardless of the struggle I was not alone.

Those few days of hopeless depression, lying alone in my "restricted" private hospital room forced me to completely reevaluate my life and its direction, or the lack thereof. Deeply repressed memories of my past and serious questions about the real causes of my present predicament made clear that my future revolved around a single decision — give up and die, or fight like hell to rewrite my destiny. Past accomplishments and successes meant nothing now. They were but small tokens of a self-deluded egotistical impression of my own self-importance. The true character of a man's life is not his possessions or meaningless accolades, but rather the blessings he brings to other people's lives through his deeds and actions. Honesty, integrity and respect are personal attributes bestowed on one's character through a life well lived and earned from others – not achieved by self-appointment! This was a lesson in life that I learned only through adversity!

2

A BROKEN HOME OF
SHATTERED LIVES

I'VE BEEN TOLD that my grand entrance into this world came early in the morning of Saturday, November 13, 1965 just after midnight. Though it was the most important day of my life, I don't remember much of anything about it! I suppose, in that respect, I'm not that different from everybody else. In hindsight it is with great thanks and a rather sobering reflection that it occurs to me my humble life may have been purely accidental.

Carolyn Rachel Ufert was nine years old when I shattered her calm world. Before I popped into the picture she was the only little Ufert playing on the family homestead in Shreveport, Louisiana. Before any preconceived notions are made I want to set the record straight. Carolyn, or "Caru" as I often called her, has always loved me the best way an older sister can, considering the whirlwind of events that rocked our family lives. Knowing the number of years that separated our births it is perhaps easier to understand why I have always believed that my birth was not planned. Yet this merely begins to set the stage for my entrance.

Even if I, Thomas Lee Ufert, had not been a planned offspring, there is little evidence that it would have caused much concern. From what I can remember of my father, Tommy, he surely would have been pleased to have a male heir. His Illinois German immigrant heritage safely confirms that fact. Furthermore, there can be no doubt of this, from the undeniable reality I was a spoiled child whom my parents loved dearly. Gloria, my mom, is said to have lavished me with her love as any mother would on her youngest child. I was the "baby". Yellowed photos from the burgeoning era of personal cameras in the mid-sixties indicate the wholesome parental love my parents had for Caru and me. I guess that is one of the reasons why it is so hard to believe that our lives were anything less than perfect. It is perhaps a way all my generation looks back at their childhood since it was so influenced by the "cookie-cutter" atmosphere of pre-Vietnam America. We were, I guess, trying to live up to that image of the perfect family. I cannot remember hearing or even knowing about families that were anything less than just like ours — perfect.

There are very few memories I have of life before age six; maybe because life really was perfect back then. Perhaps I was just so sheltered and naïve not to have realized that life is in and of itself not perfect; why should mine be so different? That pristine and innocent era of childhood is the way it should be for all children, should it not? *Yet,* I know now I am a stronger person because of the earth shattering events that affected my life. They were at least earth shattering to me, but in the full realm of life experiences, they are but shallow comparisons to the trials and tribulations of other's lives. It has taken years of personal maturity to fully comprehend *that* realization.

There is no doubt in my mind that the most influential memory of my early childhood played hand in hand with the lifelong understanding that life *is* painful. None of us are alone in that experience! I was three years old playing on the floor with my army of toys. In those days the television was contained inside a behemoth rectangular structure nearly six feet long housing also a turntable for playing LPs. Just imagine looking up from the sidewalk of a modern city at an adjacent skyscraper blocking out the sun. When you are three everything is behemoth, but nothing in our home was larger except the upright piano and the refrigerator. Needless to say the TV was a very influential part of my early years, as it has been for most American children since the early 1960s. I have known many people who can remember their *first* TV. When I was born, the TV was already there! This was the summer of 1968 and the beginning of my quest to bring peace to the world. For you see, I saw it as real then as I can still see it clearly today. An unforgettable image reached out with penetrating black & white arms from the steamy streets of Saigon. There before my eyes the Thet Offensive was as real as if in my own backyard, thanks to CBS. I, like so many other Americans, saw war firsthand, up close and personal. There were no disclaimers to shield me from the real harrowing images of that war. Even if it was black & white, the scene was real life and it forever changed mine! I saw the handcuffed and prostrated Vietcong soldier as he was — a disheveled heap of helpless humanity. Seconds later he was a mass of dead tissue with his brains and blood pouring onto the street and into my home. I saw the South Vietnamese Colonel give him a frontal lobotomy via the Smith & Wesson: I was three! Years later I came to recognize that single event as the impetus to my lifelong love for politics and international relations, especially in Asia. Several years ago I had the enlightening experience of meeting a retired Marine who briefly served under the command of that same South Vietnamese Colonel. Though he would offer few details of his Vietnamese tour of duty, perhaps for the sheer pain of remembering them, he did recount a few pertinent facts that gave me a new perspective on that event in 1968. This Marine noted, with the cool tone of so many a soldier who have seen combat, that the Vietcong had heinously slaughtered the colonel's entire family years before, and that might just explain his lack of mercy. This is just an example of what I've said before that there are three sides to every story: yours', mine, and the truth — sometimes two of them are the same. Knowing the facts about the colonel's loss doesn't necessarily excuse his actions, but it does explain the possible reasons for his behavior. As for that anonymous Marine, he only asked that I make this dedication, "From a Marine, for those who didn't make it home!"

Other than that cataclysmic memory from the TV, my early childhood seems rather normal, from what I remember. There were the typical childish aspirations to have the most toys on earth. You know how boys are, "he, who dies with the most toys, wins!" The daily Olympic accomplishment to see how long I could sit and avoid eating my vegetables, awaiting the departure of all adults, and then deviously deposit the leftovers behind the stove; this was a monumental aggravation to my parents. I truly earned every whipping for that endeavor, especially when Mom discovered the growing compost heap behind the stove! She had wondered for some time where the stench was coming from.

I had the usual kid's fascination with animals starting with "Sambo" our long eared Basset Hound, named comically after the character from Disney's *Jungle Book*. Our house seemed like the neighborhood zoo after a number of years. Between Caru and me it is a wonder our parents didn't go insane what with the gerbils, hamsters, guppies, tadpoles, kittens, Madam Queen and George! Mom had definitely said no way to a pet Boa Constrictor, but how I got away with George I'll never know! George was a baby alligator. I had delusions of grandeur training him to perform tricks and walking him through the neighborhood on a leash. Only in Louisiana! He survived the five hour car trip from Lake Charles in a shoe box. He even survived the scrawny insect meals I fed him. But George was no match for the feminine whiles of my sister and mother who had grown quite weary of his presence in a dishpan on the morning breakfast table — imagine that! I never understood their problem with seeing red peering eyes in the dark. Girls! He met his tragic fate in front of a drafty open window on an extremely cool fall morning. Though crushed from this sudden turn of events, I made sure George's farewell was proper and befitting of his place in my heart with a funeral procession, graveside service, wooden crucifix and all.

You can tell from her name that Madam Queen, my sister's cat, was certainly no nominee for Humanitarian of the Year. As my father found out, or so I was later told, Madam was a one person cat used to getting her way! This feline had a nauseating habit of using the family shower stall as her cat box. Before leaving on an unexpected trip to Houston, Dad encountered Madam's leftover goodies in a mad dash for the shower. He was so angry that he purposely left the shower doors closed, in his words, "to teach that damn cat a lesson!" For four days she would be forced to use the cat litter box, or so my father thought. Late in the evening upon their return from Houston, after an exhausting trip, Mom and Dad entered their bedroom for some much needed rest. Mom always repeated this story with much alacrity and a sense of justice, almost as if to say "the bastard got what he deserved!" It took me years to understand why. With almost premeditated and surely judicious precision, Madam Queen had defecated all over, *but only on*, Dad's side of the bed. Mom's side hadn't been touched! Dad really hated that cat. It was shortly after that, that my whole world fell apart.

The divorce, or "Big D" as I referred to it for years, came as a big surprise. It was my first of five such encounters over the next twenty years. It never appeared to me, as a small child, that my parents were having any problems. The Uferts were the typical American family — middle class, two kids, two cars living the "American dream." I was busy in my own little world of Hot Wheels race cars and life at Mrs. Body's Tinkerbelle Nursery. We lived in a nice three bedroom home at 250 East Wichita in Shreveport, Louisiana. The neighborhood was predominately white middle class and middle aged. We lived on the corner of Wichita and Holly. I still remember having arguments with

Caru that it was really "holy" street just with an extra "l". My sister and I were traditional siblings constantly arguing and irritating each other as best we could. Looking back, I'm sure it was me just being the spoiled baby and Caru trying to deal with things as best as she could. She must have heard Mom and Daddy fighting, but I don't ever remember hearing any fights. It just happened. One day Mom told us Daddy wasn't coming home anymore.

Now Daddy, a "senior" salesman for the Jim Dandy Corporation, was often away from home. I guess in those days salesmen were mostly of the traveling variety. Although to hear Mom describe it later, you'd have thought he was shacked up in a different city with some whore every weekend. A statuesque brunette of Irish descent, my mom was bitter and didn't know how else to blow off steam. If she ever believed some of the blame was her own, she never admitted it. I know too, though she never verbalized it, she always loved Tommy Ufert Senior more than she did any other man! Her eyes told it all. Daddy, though short in stature and always donning a military style flattop, was a good provider and never failed to return from his trips without presents for us. At least I guess Caru got something. I was just too preoccupied with my own little world to have ever noticed or remembered. It could also be that our seemingly gigantic age difference would not have induced in me a remarkable memory regarding a teenaged girl's gifts. That too would change.

In my mind, it was after that certain unexpected trip to Houston, when time seemed to fast forward. While our parents were away Caru and I stayed with our grandparents, Nanny and Grandpa Riley. Nanny's home was this big old house off of Southern Avenue in an area I thought for years to be called "Notary Public". A neighbor had that sign in their front yard & I misunderstood it to be the name of the neighborhood. My grandparents actually lived in a section of Shreveport known as Cedar Grove. Nanny's house had a wide rounding front porch that was fun to sit on and play. Nanny, Cleo Hickman Riley, as far as I ever knew was a simple housewife that came from a large family of 11 brothers and sisters. She was a dotting, rather short gray-haired woman who's favorite past times consisted of soap operas and chain-smoking. Grandpa, Ira Lee Riley, though I never really appreciated him for it, was a dedicated mechanic on the big 18 wheelers. The man worked hard every day of his life and did things only the way he knew how — harsh and disciplined. From my earliest childhood memories of him I don't ever remember a warm or affectionate moment. It wasn't his nature. His hands were rough like sandpaper and he regularly wore dark blue, grease stained workers pants that perfectly fit his chosen occupation. The man could easily repair any mechanical device including his pride and joy, a 1935 charcoal black Studebaker. Unlike Nanny, who spoiled me rotten, Grandpa had little patience for my habitual whining and crybaby-like demeanor. He himself, as I was to discover many years later, had been raised by a physically abusive father. Therefore, his kneejerk reaction to a surly mouthed brat like me was a swift whipping with his black leather belt or the nearest shrubbery switch he could find. He never physically abused me, but definitely believed in "hard love" as the most effective way to raise a young man. Their lives were simple and they were "salt of the earth" type people whose social activities never expanded beyond the Church of Christ, family gatherings and Grandpa's weekly attendance at the Masonic Lodge. Like in life, they loved in only the way they knew how – simple and unpretentious.

As I learned many years later, my dad had some serious heart problems. That trip to Houston was the first in a series of open heart surgeries. I've been told that heart surgery will change a man's whole life and the way he looks at his place in it. According to many, that is exactly what happened to Daddy. Though it took me almost twenty years to realize it, my dad worked hard to try and make the marriage work. Mom carried herself with an air of confidence and control portraying a physical appearance resembling a demur yet fashionable Doris Day look alike. Her hair was quaffed in the popular style of the day and she always smelled of a light baby powder aroma. In many ways my mom kept up the appearance of a happily married working woman, comparable to the female characters on the popular A&E TV series *Mad Men*. She had it all —beauty, successful marriage, promising career and a happy family home life. Appearances can be deceiving. She was never much of a housekeeper and Daddy did much of the cooking. That in and of itself explains why in later years after the divorce, I always remember Caru hating to clean house and my being so chubby. By default my sister was given the house cleaning chores and I ate whatever was fast and fattening. Remember? I hated vegetables! Where was Mom? Well, she worked for as long as I can remember as a secretary to the same man at a mortgage company. During other times she would do part time work for another small time tax accountant. In all the years I knew my mom, those were the only two jobs I can remember her having. What she loved most was bowling. That's where she and Daddy, as well as most of their friends, had met. It was a different era back then. Mom was good at it too, accomplishing placement on the state championship league team! I guess "the lanes" were her home away from home. Plenty of my time was spent there, sitting and watching if I was a good boy, or in the nursery if I was my usual bratty self.

My memories of the separation period are scant and cloudy because of the conflicting emotions that flooded my mind. I do remember visiting Daddy at his small second floor efficiency apartment on Line Avenue. The building was painted an awful dingy yellow color that conveyed a "sickly" appearance. It was fun sometimes playing on the landing outside but that pastime quickly grew old and boring. The visits were short and sometimes included trips to his girlfriend's home with her kids. There was always tension and confusion in the air. Confusion for me because there were talks of Daddy moving in with this woman and, as Caru tried to explain, having a new family. "How can he have a new family? He still has us!" There was no way for me to comprehend how that was possible. Add to this confusion, the tension of Mom's bitterness and hostility towards the woman who stole away her husband and our father. During divorces the children are usually the real victims. I went through all the stereotypical emotions: first hurt, "Doesn't he love us anymore?" Then anger, "I hate you both for wanting to break up our family!" Then shame, "I've been bad, it's my fault!" Then fear, "What will happen to us?" Then hope, "Maybe if I'm really good and do nice things to make them like each other again, Daddy will come back." Then finally to hopelessness, "I don't know what to do anymore, I feel so alone!" From the endless conversations I've had with friends over the years, these feelings from the child's perspective are similar to those who have also been through a divorce. It is so hard for the children to understand that sometimes Mommy and Daddy just don't love each other anymore. As children we see things cut and dried. " How can you not love him he's my daddy?", or "she'll do better, Daddy, you'll see!" Furthermore, many times the adults are so busy dealing with the turmoil of divorce and the *"he says, she says" bullshit*, that the fears and concerns of the kids are overlooked or lost in the shuffle.

Aunt Bobbi and Uncle Dee were Daddy's bowling friends. Though I had been to their house many times because Uncle Dee was my godfather, my recollections of them are hazy. He and Tommy were old friends. After the "big D" I don't remember them being in our lives anymore. This was the first time that people disappeared from my world in the face of adversity. One minute they were family and then they were gone. I would learn over the years to realize that people come and go through our lives with relative ease. Only through concerted efforts by both parties do people become true friends. True friendship requires no excuses or promises just love and care. After the divorce, when I was six and a half years old, many of Mom's friends became increasingly important in our lives especially the Campbell's! Joy had been one of Gloria Ufert's closest friends for years. Having first met at the bowling lanes and through other ties such as church, their affinity for each other grew and blossomed into a lifelong friendship. Mom had asked Joy to be my godmother. Thank God! Never before or since was a finer person chosen to bear such an unsung hero of a responsibility, as Joy Campbell. A devout Roman Catholic, Mrs. Campbell took her godmother duties seriously and gave the love and nurturing she would have given to her own child. She was to become the central figure in my life and thank God; she helped mold me by demonstrating how adversities build character.

Over the years I came to recognize that Joy Campbell resembled in many ways the actress Vivian Vance who played Ethel Mertz in the hit TV show *I LOVE LUCY*. Of similar build and appearance to Ethel Mertz, she was a fierce and dynamic friend who could often be very opinionated and never backed down from anyone or anything. Her devotion to friend and family knew no limitations and she could easily be described as fearless. For as long as I knew and loved Joy Campbell, no word describes her better than absolutely heroic.

Some of Mom's other friends included Dudley, Andrea, and Martha. Dudley was one of Mom's friends that would remain so for life. Until many years later I would know little of him or his invaluable friendship. My early memories consisted of an unusual fellow, tall and lanky, who made infrequent appearances at "the lanes." Andrea Bowles was more of a friend of a friend. Introduced to Mom by Mrs. Campbell, Andrea also would become a lifelong, yet fiercely honest and realistic friend. She never "beat around the bush" and always called things as she saw them. No finer qualities can one ask for in a true friend. They tell you *what you need to hear*, not *what you want to hear*. One final person should be mentioned, Martha. Martha was a delight of a woman in many respects. I think that Mom liked her a lot because Martha made her laugh. Hell, Martha made everyone laugh and was a good drinking buddy. Mom and Martha liked their beers. The lady was a jovial and robust woman who made her living as a sales rep for a popular local highline jewelry store. She was a good friend *while the times were good*. She cared about my mom, I have no doubt. However, like so many people in our lives, when times get rough, you discover who your true friends are.

Divorce is hardest on the children. In my lifetime single parent households have become commonplace. The psychological and emotional trauma for children in a divorce ravaged home can be devastating, especially during the formative years of ages five through ten. This was certainly the case for me. Home life suddenly lacked structure and consistency for any of us. Though we can be quite resilient and adapt remarkably well as children growing up in a broken home, the deep seeded effects can lie dormant for years revealing only shrouded clues that are often easily dismissed or ignored. The combination of my father's traveling occupation and the subsequent divorce resulted in a childhood lacking in a strong positive male influence. In many cases a diminished fatherly influence can be easily overcome. However, my situation was not to be so.

Times had been truly rough for the last several years and my mom's solution was to go on vacation! Florida, here we come!

3

VACATION & RELOCATION
DO NOT BRING SALVATION

LIFE WAS OKAY. We were going to make it. All we needed was to get away for a while and relax. Fun and sun would make all our lives easier to take. So Florida it was. Florida was going to save us from all of the gloom in our lives. Not! Back then I believed in fairy tales especially when adults told me so. Florida just proved that you can't run away from your problems. Maybe you can hide for a while, but sooner or later you will run into them again. It's almost as if life wants you to learn a lesson whether you want to or not. Nonetheless, we were going to have some fun to help us forget our troubles.

Mom, Martha, Caru, and I loaded into the maroon Plymouth and set out on my greatest adventure yet. We were going to Pensacola and the beach. No trip east would be complete without stopping to see Aunt Jan and the gang in Jackson, Mississippi. First however, we had to cross over the Mississippi River on the old bridge. This was perhaps the only time during the entire trip that Caru and I were not at each other's throats. We were told that if we made too much noise as we crossed over the old bridge it would collapse, and we would go tumbling to our certain deaths for hungry alligators awaited below. Mom and Martha made the most of that short respite, for as usual, Caru and I had been asking every 5 minutes for the last several hundred miles, "Are we there yet? Are we there yet?"

My Mississippi cousins were fun and scary all at the same time. Everyone had someone to entertain them and show them the sites. Mom and Martha would spend their time talking late into the night with Aunt Jan. She was as close to a sister as my mom had ever come. Jan had also suffered through a divorce and worked hard to raise her four children alone. My aunt Jan, like mom, was rather tall and dark headed though slightly more slender. In my mind, primarily because of her beautiful smile and boisterous laugh, she was probably my most favorite adult relative. Trouble never seemed to darken her door, though I realize now that her good natured temper and contagious good humor were in many ways a defensive camouflage to protect her and her children from life's hard knocks.

My sister would chatter and cackle all night long with our cousin Betty. Both were in their mid teens and had hair, rock and roll, and boys on the brain to keep them up all night long. That left yours truly in the very capable hands of my cousins Tim, John, and Harry. You can only imagine the mischief four adolescent boys were bound to mix up. As I said before my cousins were fun *and* scary. The boys were fun because we got into fireworks, hide and seek, war games, playing tricks on our sisters, etc; yet, they scared me something fierce. To this day I am still horrified by the mere memory of one of their freakish pranks; chasing through the dark they would terrorize me with the site of their eyelids turned inside out like freakish zombies from the dead. Harry and I being the youngest were the usual targets of this treachery. Betty too, was scary if for no other reason than the infamous hairbrush. If we pesky boys bugged our sisters too much then we would be threatened with a beating with a hard plastic handle hairbrush, and that was a terror worse than death as far as we were concerned. All in all though, we had a blast in Jackson. I remember most fondly the midnight junkets to Krystal Burgers; they were a must for every trip we made to visit our Mississippi cousins. Most of our infrequent visits were stopovers lasting only the night or maybe a whole weekend. Looking back I realize that my times in Jackson were some of the most fun times of all my childhood because they were just that — childish fun with no care in the world. Aunt Jan was a strong woman with determination and love that knew no bounds. There can be no doubt that Mom was in serious need of that strength; she certainly hungered for Jan's advice and counsel on this particular trip. She knew that if there was anyone she could trust and would empathize with her situation it would be Jan. After all she had already been through the hell of divorce and survived with her family intact. All I really remember was horsing around with my cousins, eating Krystal burgers, annoying our older female siblings, and having to eat disgusting Captain Crunch for breakfast — yuck! I couldn't wait to play in the ocean.

We left early the next day and headed for Florida. We arrived later that evening and checked into our beachside hotel. I was so excited I could not sleep. At the crack of dawn I was scampering to comb the beach. Those six days in Fort Lauderdale were pretty much the same. My activities basically included building sand castles, trying to catch any marine life possible, splashing in the salty water of the Gulf of Mexico, and obtaining the best Tan of my life, before or since! Naturally blonde, my hair was almost white by the time we departed. There was not a single day that didn't find little Thomas Ufert out and about in the sun and surf. Ironically, I was and still am slightly afraid of the water.

Caru on the other hand, had developed horrible sunburn on the first or second day. I can't remember which, just that she was miserable the entire time. Granted she was in pain and her attitude was in sure need of adjustment, but what did I care. It was her fault for getting burned, wasn't it? I'd been outside every day, all day, and wasn't screaming in pain like a little girl. As children we can be so cruel and heartless. Furthermore, Caru was plunged into additional misery by having to baby sit me so Mom and Martha could go shopping! Naturally all I wanted was to play outside — the last thing my sister wanted to do! It was a hopeless impasse.

As a matter of self-preservation the adults had a plan. Mom and I would go to Sea World, and Martha would take Caru shopping. I actually knew nothing of where we were going. Mom said it was a big surprise and I should be on my best behavior. The trip would take about two hours. I was restless and excited. The route was pretty much the same for those two hours. There was sand as far as my little eyes could see. Sand and more sand! The combined excitement and restlessness would normally have resulted in my behaving like an unbearable brat. But not today!

Suddenly there was smoke coming from under the hood of our car! It almost scared me into urinating in my pants. I had never seen anything like it and knew for sure the Plymouth was on fire, would explode, and we would be blown to bits. Yet Mom's reassuring voice consoled me. As she began to pull the car over I felt confident that no matter what happened my mom would protect me. Her voice was loving but serious and conveyed an air of no nonsense. For the first time in my young life I remember coming to grips with danger. This event has remained with me ever since, probably because never before had I felt like "the man of the family." Not once did I pause or question her orders. It just seemed natural, at such a serious juncture, for me to behave. I do recall worrying for Mom and knowing that I would do anything she asked simply because danger was at hand. There was no way to protect her if I was playing around; those were my thoughts. In reality how could I, a seven year old, possibly protect her?

In those days passersby would stop and offer assistance without fear of being carjacked. One did. Our car was towed to a nearby gas station and repaired. I think Mom was overjoyed as well surprised with my excellent behavior. Being such a spoiled baby, past experience had certainly demonstrated a lack of discipline on my part. She praised me over and over for "being such a good boy." That made my surprise all the sweeter. Mom decided that I had earned the right to know where we were going. It wasn't until we arrived at Sea World that my excitement surged out of control. Firstly, I was still somewhat in shock over our "near death" car fire. Secondly, my only real frame of reference to the wonders of this theme park was the TV show "Flipper" (now I'm showing my age!) I had the time of my young life!

This small digression is significant because it truly cemented, in my mind, our relationship. Those two "dangerous" hours together, just Mom and I, were unique and never again to be repeated with such euphoria. To this day I can look back on that experience as the happiest time of my early childhood. With the divorce totally rocking my world and the trauma that was soon to follow, our trip to Sea World was monumental. It is just such memories that can bring smiles years later when it seems your world is crumbling. You survived then and you'll survive now to be blessed with even greater memories if one only doesn't give up hope. Our memories, good and bad, are ours and serve to provide the necessary fluffy cushion we all need from time to time. No matter how bad life got over the years, my memory of that trip to Sea World always brought me a smile. I have heard these moments in our lives referred to as "Happy Places" that keep us alive and young at heart. Though significant in my early childhood, this trip to Sea World was but one of a handful of moments in my life that could qualify. For most people, including myself, *the* Happy Place tends to be a singular memory totally free of want or care. This is an undeniable truth I am sure most can relate to. Many years would pass before *my Happy Place* would occur and many more before I was wise enough to recognize it.

*   *   *   *

Don Adams was a Tech Sgt. In the United States Air Force stationed at nearby Barksdale Air Force Base. He seemed likable enough; at least my mom liked him — *liked him a lot*. I remember Don to be a big man who just seemed to tower over me. Daddy had not been as looming. Don was tall, muscular and almost gruff like a grizzly bear. In my memory it seems that he appeared on the scene shortly after we returned from Florida. More likely he and Mom had met several months earlier, I guess at the bowling lanes. That was usually where Mom met many of her friends. However this friend was different. He seemed to be spending more and more time at our house. In fact, he and Mom had sort of a whirlwind romance. Like so many children of divorce, I resented this new presence in my environment. I *was* going to write that I disliked him because he was firm and commanded discipline, not because I thought he was trying to replace my dad. After 29 years the realization has just hit that I did resent him for trying to be my daddy. I distinctly remember refusing his orders by saying, "I don't have to obey you; you're not my dad!" Of course, being in the military my rebuff of his authority was not well received. He was used to having his orders followed without question. This would be the core of our mutual dislike for each other.

It was so sudden. One day I'm with Mom visiting Don at the base, and then I was part of the small wedding party at Barksdale's generic ecumenical church. Mom explained that since Don wasn't Roman Catholic, they had decided to have the wedding on base. It wasn't until years later that I realized because of her divorce the church would not allow her to remarry. Mom had always been devout in her faith; she had rejected her parents' religion, the Church of Christ, and had raised us as Catholic. So I know now that this was a major compromise for her. She sacrificed so much — her hometown, her faith, her occupational independence, even her daughter. All of this was done for the security and stability that the marriage was supposed to provide.

I am sure too, that her children's welfare was a major concern.

The divorce had affected her severely and resulted in my seeing a child psychiatrist. Now, years later, I suspect that Mom was concerned about me for many reasons. Close family friends have confided that she and others regarded my behavior as "abnormal" in many respects. To be granted the divorce certainly played a major role in some of these. However, all totaled Mom felt that a child therapist might be of some much-needed help.

The car trips to the doctor's office off North Market were lengthy and subdued. He was a therapist and wanted me to think of him as a "friend." He did have lots of toys to play with while we talked. I especially liked the plastic dinosaurs. That is the extent of my memories from those sessions. I do not even remember his name. Those hours seemed to drag on and on each week. I have never discovered the result, if any, of his diagnosis. Those same family friends have noted that my mom was greatly concerned with my sometimes almost violent temper tantrums and keen interest in playing with dolls. I suppose the latter was the earliest sign of things to come. Mrs. Campbell admitted years later that she and Mom had discussed the subject, with a confession of a family secret that there was "a known tendency" in the family. If so, I never knew it or realized it.

Nevertheless, it makes perfect sense that Mom sought out a strong male figure to support her and her family. That is the only explanation to be found for her next big decision. Today we call it "relocation." When I was a kid it simply was "were moving." Originally from Tuscaloosa, Alabama, Don Adams decided he wanted to return to familiar surroundings upon his discharge from the Air Force. That was fine for Don but it wrecked the Ufert household.

My entire life had been spent at the house on Wichita and Holly. Endless days, it seemed, had been given over the years to the great family pastime of raking up leaves… and pine straw — it was absolutely everywhere! Four massive pine trees sat in our front yard and several more stood in the back yard; every nook and cranny of that yard found a way to collect pine straw, so it was a never ending battle. That house had seen many a Christmas Eve party with family and friends. It was the biggest event of the year for our household. There were rum cakes and fudge, Chex party mix, chips and dips, punch; you name it; it was on the dining room table that night. Someone would be playing Christmas carols on the huge upright piano, grownups were everywhere. The tree stood in the front window corner and had many different luminescent ornaments. Those evenings alone were of enough sentimental value to make thinking of moving an absolute horror.

I didn't have many friends in the neighborhood, not my age anyway. My little two square block world was populated mostly by middle-aged retirees. There were the Godbys, the Whitelys, the Paynes, and Mrs. Mattingly. Come to think of it, there wasn't one kid my age whose name I remember. The kids were there, *somewhere*. Like most children, as I got older my world expanded. I discovered a group of "urchins" who usually played on Saturdays. Having been given a policeman's costume for Christmas one year, I always portrayed a cop when we played cops and robbers. For years I just knew that what I wanted most was to grow up and be a policeman. Boy! That dream changed fast. Perhaps my point has become lost, but for a seven year old boy, that home was everything. It represented all I knew. Even now, almost thirty years later driving past that house pulls heartstrings like no other building can. Don was taking that away from me and Mom was letting him!

My feelings were compounded by the fact that my sister didn't have to go. She was staying in Shreveport, with Nanny and Grandpa, to complete her last few years of high school at St. Vincent's Academy. The entire ordeal was traumatic. However, the worst was yet to come. New dad, okay. New city and state, I'll live. New house… you make do. New school, oh my God! Talk about a fate worse than death. Not only was I the new kid in school, but these kids "talked funny!" This was truly "the heart of Dixie."

Not since kindergarten had I been to public school. There were no uniforms, and that was kind of cool. Yet many things were really different, like the size of the school. It was twice as big as St. John's. The whole move left me in a clouded state. Everything seemed gray and dreary — the city, the school, the neighborhood, our house. Looking back, it is easier for me to understand how adult decisions can really screw up kids' lives, no matter how good intentioned they might be. For me there was nothing positive to remember about moving to Alabama.

Don had finished his service commitment to the USAF and bought a home back in Tuscaloosa. There was little doubt that this place was originally intended to be a bachelor's pad. My room didn't even have a door on it, just some oriental style sheet hanging in the doorway. Don must have gotten it while on a tour of duty in the Far East. It seemed the honeymoon ended upon our arrival. Early on things didn't feel right. We met Don's relatives, the air felt stilted… polite, but stilted. His family wasn't rude or pretentious, the atmosphere just felt odd. Mom and I were "strangers in a strange land." Marital tension loomed once again throughout the house and it seemed to permeate the very air I breathed. The beaming smile Mom had worn on her wedding day and even the day we arrived in Tuscaloosa had vanished.

Our adventure to Alabama lasted less than six months. Its toll on Mom was far more severe. Don may have been loud and overbearing, but he had not been physically abusive. The humiliation on Mom's character and ego were the hardest hit victims.

She had allowed her insecurity and need for a husband to quash any thoughts of a long engagement. Don was in many ways a rebound for my mother. Like we all discover in relationships, dating someone and living with them are two completely different worlds. In the end I don't think either of them was upset to be splitting up. Don was certainly more domineering and belligerent than Mom had ever anticipated. She did not become the doting housewife whom Don had envisioned for himself. It just didn't work!

Me? Well like most kids, I could bend. Hell, I was thrilled to be going home again. There was nothing or no one I would miss from this tired hick town. Remember I was only 7 ½, now. My world had been uprooted; I had been separated from friends and family, thrown into a completely strange environment, and re-encountered familial discord. It was only natural to view everything in my world as dark and distasteful. Returning to Shreveport would be the happiest thing that had happened since being splashed by "Flipper." I was relieved the nightmare had ended so quickly.

Before the age of eight, divorce had twice rocked my world. Though I would experience similar repercussions three more times in my life, these first two home wrecking episodes would lay the foundation for many of my own failed relationships in the future. I firmly believe the seeds of distrust, infidelity, poor self esteem and immediate gratification were sowed into my subconscious during those formative years. In fact to this day I can point to only one relationship that was not plagued by doubts of success. My life experiences seemed to prove beyond a shadow of doubt that true love was fleeting and doomed to failure. Have faith! I am living proof that unconditional love does exist and usually where you least expect it, typically because of your own foolish stupidity.

In hindsight this brief but traumatic episode proves that sacrificing all you believe in and hold dear, for the sake of security, is far too great a price to pay. In the end you've gained nothing and sold your soul for a pittance. Following foolish dreams in the hope of a better life happens to us all. Failing to learn from our mistakes, or taking the easy way out, never ends in success. On the contrary we usually find ourselves mired in a quagmire of bad habits that can only lead to despair and hopeless capitulation.

4

THIEF IN THE NIGHT

IT WAS CHRISTMAS. The backseat of the car was full of wrapped presents. There was no way I could survive the entire two day trip without opening them. Tuscaloosa, Alabama, had been dark and gloomy. That's at least how I remembered it. The six month stay had been a fiasco. For Mom it had been a humiliation and she was now returning home "with her tail between her legs." Her second marriage was a failure and she had to ask her parents for help. Looking back now the whole trip home was filled with an eerie silence. Other than an overnight stay with my clan of cousins in Jackson, Mississippi, our homecoming seemed dark and foreboding. Little did I know what future lay ahead!

*   *   *   *

Ira and Cleo Riley, affectionately known as Nanny and Grandpa, were hard working people from humble origins. There was nothing pretentious about them. Grandpa had spent his life earning a respectable living as a big rig mechanic. I am sad to admit I know little of their origins other than Grandpa hailed originally from Texas and Nanny came from the Hickman clan of Tennessee. Grandpa at times could be a hard task master showing little emotion especially with regards to a spoiled child such as me. Nanny on the other hand was as loving and cherishing as any grandmother. In fact I could usually "get away with murder" in her eyes. Being common people they lived life simply, requiring none of the trappings of wealth or station. My biological grandparents loved each other dearly and did their best to share that, as they only knew how. Not until decades later, after their deaths, did I fully understand this fact.

Nanny and Grandpa had taken in my sister, Caru, upon Mom's second marriage. Thinking clearly of Caru's best interests they offered to look after her so that she could complete her remaining years of high school. Otherwise she would have been forced to transfer to a public school in Alabama forgoing opportunities otherwise unavailable to her. My biological grandparents are certainly to be commended for this unselfish endeavor. They were by no means young people attempting to care for a teenage girl in her prime. Continuing her private school education was essential.

Even after our return home Caru continued to reside with Nanny and Grandpa at their home on LakeHearst Street. Mom and I lived in a small two bedroom home only a few blocks away on Canal Street. Fortunately, Mom was able to resume her secretarial duties at the mortgage company she had left previously. I resumed my studies at St. John Berchman's grade school. It was midterm of my third grade year. The utter shakeup of my family life, the total upheaval of moving, and the renewed spousal tension of Mom's second marriage had left me a rather unruly child, even more so than before.

Returning to Mrs. Karam's class brought some familiarity because of seeing friendly classmates and the old haunts of my school. However, the third grade was where I can honestly say trouble began. I was a member of the "seven up club". That was a reference to Mrs. Karam's seven after school regulars. We were the cut ups that, in addition to regular homework, had endless pages of dictionary words to copy — our usual punishment for misbehaving in class or failing to complete assignments.

In those days misbehaving generally involved talking during class, shooting spit wads, passing notes, or our regular favorite of thumping paper footballs across the room. We would certainly be considered mild mannered compared to the exploits of drugs, abuse, and violence so prevalent today. We were not bad kids, just in need of some discipline. I found out years later that each of us was encountering problems at home.

*   *   *   *

Multiple sclerosis or MS as it is commonly referred to today, was like some thief in the night. It came and stole my mother away. I don't know that I really understood anything about this sickness until many years later. All I knew was that things were changing; *I didn't know why* and *I didn't know how* to change things back. Even worse, I didn't know that I couldn't change things back! My first real encounter with MS was somewhat terrifying.

Mom and I were driving in the maroon Plymouth. It was dark. Mom turned to enter a strip shopping mall. I was too short to see over the dashboard without standing. In those days seatbelts were so passé. Suddenly there was a sudden bump, a loud screeching and grating sound and the car stopped dead. Mom cursed out loud. She tried to put the car in reverse or even to put it back in drive. It would not move at all. She had missed the driveway into the parking lot and driven over a large curb, scraping the underside of the car. Mom lost her nerve and began to cry emotionally. She wasn't as upset about the car as she was to realize that her failing eyesight had caused the entire incident; a fact I was too young to appreciate. That was the beginning of her long arduous struggle with MS.

As with so many debilitating diseases, they affect not only the patient, but also everyone they come in contact with. MS affects one physically, emotionally, and psychologically. In the mid-1970s little was known about this tragic illness. Doctors certainly could predict its known symptoms, but so little else. Their treatment and prognosis were sketchy at best. This fact only contributed further to the seemingly hopeless situation Mom faced. I can't even begin to imagine the cascade of doom she must have felt was laid upon her already weighted shoulders. Within two short years she had suffered two failed marriages and subsequent divorces; uprooted her life, relocated, and been forced to cower home in defeat; suffer the agonizing realization that in the prime of her life she was rapidly transformed from vibrant independence to dependent subsistence; and finally the knowledge that she could no longer provide the adequate care and security for an adolescent child. The human spirit is an enduring phenomenon, but one never knows how much they can take. In many ways your view of the world and how others receive you, can exert an immeasurable influence on how you deal with your circumstances. I am truly in awe of my mother's stamina to have dealt with so much and remained as determined as she was. *It was a lesson that has served me well ever since.*

Initially she coped with great courage and conviction. Her doctors prescribed a regimen of exercise and medication. She began with a long black cane and did her best to walk as independently as possible. She attempted to keep her job, but to no avail. For Gloria Ufert, MS was quick and devastating. Previous years of drinking beer while taking valium had certainly weakened her neuromuscular system to aid the illness' progression. I certainly can't remember how many weeks or months it took. All I do know is that it started when I was about eight years old and by the time I was ten she could not walk without a walker.

Children adapt remarkably well to change in many ways; not so for many adults. Change can be a subtle destroyer of happiness and dreams, for both children and adults. Mom's illness had affected her in a noticeable way. I was too young to realize its effects upon me. The human spirit makes great strides and overcomes many obstacles to care for the ones we love in order to survive. You do things *because they just need to be done* and don't stop to ask why. In many cases one doesn't have time to stop and ask why or even reflect upon the issues at hand. In addition to being just a child, I guess that explains why I never questioned the rapidly changing nature of my relationship with my mother. It never occurred to me to question if a nine year old child should be doing most of the laundry, cooking, and cleaning. Let there be no doubt my efforts were a feeble attempt, but *you do what you have to do*. Mom could *not* do it. There seemed to be no one else around.

Though they lived only blocks away, Nanny and Grandpa were not there from day to day. He worked and worked very hard. Nanny took care of me after school. I can't remember her doing much else except constantly smoking and watching "her shows."

I have no doubt that they loved my mom. She was their only child; however, their seeming act of negligence would affect our relationship for years to come. Mom had always strived to survive without her parents. I'll never really know why she was bound and determined to keep their influence to a minimum, but that was certainly her intention. Far too many times over the years she had tried to control their encroachments into her life and that of her children. This attitude undoubtedly played a major role in our family drama. Nonetheless, it would be decades before any clarity would become evident, and then only after most of the parties involved were dead. What a shame.

This also was how I saw my sister. Mom's attempts to control her own parents influence over Caru, for whatever reason, had strained *their* mother/daughter relationship. What I remember of their "falling out" is trivial compared to the actual results of their fight. It was years later before they really spoke to each other again. Like so many arguments I'm not even sure anyone remembers what caused it. Being strong willed women trying to deal with the circumstances which were affecting all our lives, it was inevitable they would come to blows. The rather small dent in the wall where Caru pushed Mom would serve as a reminder for years to come.

Caru had decided that her only escape from the tragedy was to marry. I remember that she and Mom been at odds for years; however, her decision to marry Austin Davis, a coworker from Vivian, Louisiana, was the climax. Mom felt that Caru was making a big mistake and surely did not want her daughter to make the same errors she had made herself. My sister was in love and thought it was her only way out. Mom's illness had not quite progressed to the point of incapacity, but it had certainly begun to affect her psychologically. Caru's refusal to accept Mom's advice was yet another example of a growing betrayal that Mom felt everyone around her was party to. I also would have my part to play in this "conspiracy."

The feeling of betrayal would last for years to come. Mom's fixation on that small dent in the wall served as a daily reminder. For me, Caru's escape could only be categorized as abandonment; I felt completely left alone to care for my mother, and myself. That fateful feeling would last for years to come and probably serve as the main reason for my refusal to accept and love my sister as fully as I should have. Although there were innumerable influences on the lack of sibling love between us, this one in particular I saw as the primary. If I had any regrets in my life, this would be the greatest. Only at our mother's funeral some ten years later would Caru and I ever become close, and that was short lived.

Many specialists point to traumatic childhood experiences as cornerstones in the development of lifelong animosities. My feeling of abandonment certainly is the foundation of my distant feelings toward my biological family. Whether or not that is right or wrong, simply put it is the reality. Only after years of growth and maturity, as well as hindsight, can I honestly put this in perspective. There is no fault to be laid on anyone's shoulders; however, laying fault elsewhere is usually the easiest road to choose. It is rare in the face of adversity that one looks in the mirror first. We usually prefer to cast that heavy cloak in other directions. Unfortunately that can be said of many families. The ones we love are usually the closest and easiest targets for our anger. Over the years I have found few families that fit the "Cleavers." As I shall detail later, events soon transpire that would wedge further and further distance between us all.

*   *   *   *

My efforts to do anything and everything possible for Mom stood no limits. But as a small boy one can only do so much. Furthermore, those efforts dealt primarily with the physical world around me. Third, fourth, and fifth grades were very rough; dealing with the troubles at home only made life at school more difficult, both personally and academically. I'm no whiz kid. I've been blessed with average intelligence. School has always been hard work for me. That fact was only compounded by the drama unfolding at home. My problems there shrouded everything else. My attention span in school was short and easily distracted. There are few words to adequately describe me in grade school; however, reflecting back, weird and "nerdy" come to mind. I had the extremely bad habit of wearing my uniform shirt buttoned to the top button. I was chubby. I enjoyed singing and music class. My athletic prowess and interest in sports were almost nonexistent; efforts at kickball and handball were not stellar by any means. There was no strong male influence in my life to encourage such things. My thoughts always seemed to wander in other areas such as history and famous people. All of these attributes combined made me a prime target for jeering and ridicule. Most of the guys in my class teased me. I had noticed over time that the girls used a very successful weapon to deter the boys from pestering them; they would blow kisses at them. When we are young there is a period where the opposite sex revolts us and we find them just… weird. Granted, for most kids that situation doesn't last long.

The girls were quite successful; blowing kisses just seemed to make the boys run away. Well, it worked for them, why not me? Or so I thought. That decision would live to haunt me for at least ten years or more. Most of the guys I went to grade school with would also become my classmates at Jesuit High School. Some of the older boys would never let me forget, even through college. With problems at home and my own struggle to pass in school, anything that would stop the bullying was worth a shot. It never occurred to me that my actions would be regarded as anything more than a defense mechanism. From my perspective, the price was worth it. My physical stature was not befitting of a jock or bully, so fighting wasn't an option. As far as my classmates were concerned I was a sissy.

During fifth grade I was beginning to discover the numerous changes known as puberty. My family life involved Mom, Caru, Nanny, and Grandpa — three women and one man. Because Grandpa worked all day the women played a dominant role in my daily life. Grandpa could be such a stern task master that our relationship rarely found a fond footing. In many ways, without real just cause, I was afraid of him. The point is that my environment was not conducive to the flourishing of a "cool dude." All the really cool guys, even in grade school, seemed to follow that other path, the heavily traveled one. Nothing about me seemed to be "normal" or at least not like the majority of my male peers. Only in my neighborhood did I find "fellas" of a similar breed. Not "sissies" but rather more academically minded. I wasn't a sissy either, just using the likeness of such to avoid endless bullying, which in the end created a vicious cycle. I hid behind the sissy persona to stop the bullies but ended up adding fuel to the fire. Many years later one classmate would complement me by saying, "Tom I never thought you'd turn out okay, but you have come a long way, for the better!" Thanks Tracy N.

I was very fortunate growing up. Attending private school during the era of the 1970's and 1980's, my "sissy" demeanor was not subjected to the cruel and even deadly bullying so common in today's schools. I was the brunt of incessant verbal and attitudinal ridicule, but that behavior never became physical or violent. I grew up in a different time and in a different social environment proceeding the contemporary era where homophobic physical and psychological abuse is more prevalent. However, the jeering I did receive affected me deeply resulting in a sense of paranoia that made me feel like a social outcast. Typically I was a loner with few close friends and was generally regarded as a weirdo. This traumatic experience caused a severe detriment to my social skills and self-esteem. It would take years of concentrated effort, on my part and that of many adults in my life, to reverse the effects. The major lesson I learned was that survival and acceptance often require a "behavior modification" that can have a long term negative impact on one's mental health. Peer pressure is an extremely powerful force on a child's character development that can last a lifetime.

*   *   *   *

It must've been a weekend, for I was home doing something in my room. The washer and dryer were going and Mom was sitting on the sofa watching TV. Her walker was close at hand. Over the last several months her condition had grown worse. The household chores had fallen pretty much in my lap. She did try to help but it was just so frustrating for her and me. Like so many people, I guess, it was just easier for me to do what I could and not ask or expect her to help. Grandpa would mow the yard and make any repairs we required. He and Nanny would help transport me with the groceries from the store. The vacuuming, dishwashing, dusting, laundry, and cooking had become almost routine chores for me. I tried hard, but at age nine a child doesn't have the experience or knowledge to do these things first rate.

In addition Mom needed my assistance. There were times when she was unable to reach the bathroom or even make it out of bed in time to perform normal bodily functions. For the person who is ill, urinating and defecating on oneself is bad enough; having to ask someone else to clean you, especially your nine year old son, is perhaps the most humiliating experience for our so fragile egos. There was never a time that I helped Mom with this that she didn't cry. For the loved one helping, the experience is both humbling and demoralizing. You want to help because you love them; you know they want to do it on their own. Your heart silently screams, for you see the degradation flooding their eyes; and you know that they hate to ask but they have no choice. Years would pass before I myself had to endure this, but I can honestly empathize, not just sympathize.

There is no measuring stick for the amount of humiliation required to make one snap. Even through all of my trials and tribulations, I consider myself blessed for they have never broken me. I have Mom to thank. In a single desperate act (one that I've never written or spoken of in any detail before now) I witnessed the source of my life, all that I loved and lived for; want nothing more than to die. She taught me in a single moment the true value of life: *Love*.

Walking into the din I found my mom slumped over the arm of the sofa. A pill bottle had fallen from her shaking hands onto the linoleum floor, scattering the few remaining capsules everywhere. "Mama! Mama! Wake up! What's wrong? What have you done?" I grabbed her and tried in vain to shake her awake. She was groggy and incoherent. I screamed and yelled for help. No one heard me. Of course there was no one to hear me. Even in her groggy state she pleaded for me just to go away. Knowing my grandparents' house was but a few blocks away, I told Mom not to worry and that help would soon be there. She weakly reached for my arm to stop me but I broke away and ran as fast as I could. For some reason, probably the horror of the moment, using the telephone never occurred to me. The night was dark like the nightmare

I was living. Frantically running the five blocks to my grandparents I burst into their home some ten minutes later. Breathless and deranged, I tried to explain what I had seen. Nanny held and comforted her sobbing grandchild, while Grandpa hurriedly dressed and drove to my house.

Shortly thereafter Grandpa called. I just knew Mom was dead. Thank God I was wrong. After pumping her stomach the hospital kept my mother a few days for observation. I stayed with my grandparents and went to school on Monday. Everyone assured me that my mom was going to be okay. Over the last several months I had been in contact with Mrs. Campbell, my godmother and my mom's best friend. She had made every effort to keep in touch with Gloria and check up on me. Joy Campbell had assured me that her door was always open and I could call her at any time. Little did I know how true to her word she would be!

Grandpa picked me up from school as always. That Monday had been morose and left me feeling fearful of the future that lay ahead. My thoughts drifted all day and even the slightest gibe from anyone sent me into a flood of tears. Though I'm sure the faculty were all aware of the previous weekend's events, my classmates must have surely just brushed off my behavior as more sissy drama. That evening at home, alone with Mom, would make my day at school feel like a circus parade.

Grandpa and I walked into the somber Canal Street house. I wasn't sure what to expect. My thoughts were jumbled between exaltation that my mom was okay and the fear of the unknown. Fear that somehow everything had now changed. Would she try again? What would happen to me if she succeeded? In the end my love for her and the joy that she was still alive helped me run eagerly to see her. She sat in her usual spot on the sofa in the den. Her color was ghostly white and you could almost feel her physical agony. I reached to hug Mom but was warned that the stomach pump had left her severely sore and weak. Grandpa left after a few minutes to fetch Mom's new prescriptions, announcing that he would return shortly.

Her once beautiful azure blue eyes now glared at me steely for several minutes as she remained stoically quiet. I stressed how happy I was to see her and that she was okay. She began to cry. I will never forget the next few minutes for the rest of my life. In her sobbing state she said to me, "I hate you! Why couldn't you just let me die?" Back then I was just too young to understand how she felt or why. Those words seared through me like none before or since. As you will see this event would serve as the foundation for my thoughts many years later when Mom died.

A plastic gold colored crucifix hung over my bed. That night began a ritual that continued for a very long time. In the darkness of my small room I would stand and kiss the head of Christ and beg for his mercy. I knew nowhere else to turn and had little hope of any reprieve from my prison. In my heart there was hope and faith that all of this would turn out okay. My mind couldn't see how. My story is living proof that God does work in mysterious ways, miracles do happen, and Angels are among us. These are true realities for us all; if we would take the time to see them and keep our hearts open to them.

Watching a loved one lose all hope and doubt the value of their own life is an unbearable experience for anyone, especially a young child. Even more traumatic was the unforgettable searing image of my own mother glaring at me and expressing her seemingly genuine hatred for the act of saving her life. Mom's irredeemably forsaken demeanor ripped through my heart like a piece of jagged glass! From this experience I learned that the human spirit can not be saved by even the deepest expression of love when it has reached a point of no return in total despair. Only the sheer will to live knowing that you have a purpose and your life has meaning can pull you from the darkest recesses of adversity.

5

A SECOND CHANCE

A SECOND CHANCE...JOY and Charles Campbell with their son Chuck and his wife Karen were mine. Not only was Joy Campbell my mom's best friend but more importantly to me she was my godmother. I had enjoyed many visits to her home, numerous encounters at the bowling lanes and infrequent shopping trips with her throughout my childhood. Few people in this world have taken their godparent responsibilities as seriously as Joy Campbell. For her it wasn't just a duty but more of a love, as it should be. Even today, some 46 years after my birth, no human being has been there for me more than she. I cannot point to *anyone* who has been there from day one to this very day, but Joy Campbell. That statement carries no judgment; it is just simple fact. This perhaps explains our special relationship and underlines our unending love for each other. My life has been truly blessed by her never ending presence and loving influence. No accolade, award, or honor could adequately endow her with the praise she so rightly deserves. My only prayer is that she knows my love for her and that it may suffice as enough reward.

At this time I must make a rather sad editorial note that while writing and refining the final draft of this book Mrs. Joy Campbell passed away. She alone deserves credit as the driving force behind the writing and subsequent completion of this endeavor.

Although she has left our earthly confines her presence and memory are felt daily now that she has joined my mom as one of my most inspirational and guiding guardian angels.

Joy and Charles Campbell were a relatively happy couple as were their son, Chuck, and his wife Karen. Happiness is such a relative term and its form is forever changing. Perhaps that is why for so many it is such a fleeting possession. In my eyes the Campbell's world was a far cry from mine. Success, love, and happiness had provided the material comforts, as well as the means to maintain, what most of us seek. One's perspective can be easily clouded; in retrospect my world really wasn't that bad.

Having originally met and married in Ferriday, Louisiana, Joy and Charles set about to raise a family and live life as best they could. They eventually left that small town and moved to Shreveport. Over the years they became accustomed to a simple yet comfortable lifestyle. They had worked hard in their respective careers and succeeded in surviving. Joy worked for over 20 years as the sole assistant to a well-respected dentist. Charles worked tirelessly in a rather menial position for a life and casualty insurance company. They provided a good stable home for Chuck and were fortunate to be able to send him to St. John's College Prep, that in 1964 was renamed Jesuit High School (now known as Loyola College Prep). Like most of us these were good hard working people doing their best the only way they knew how.

After graduating, Chuck then attended night school to become an x-ray technician. Chuck was a big man, measuring around 6 foot one, with broad shoulders and a boyish face. He had struggled through school. He was blessed with more common sense than book sense. More importantly, he wasn't ashamed to admit it and constantly sought to try and improve himself. Marrying Karen Bolte was certainly a step in

41

that direction. Also in the medical field, a registered nurse anesthetist or RNA, Karen had met Chuck while working at the same hospital. Originally from Erie, Pennsylvania, she came from a rather cultured family of musicians. She herself was an accomplished violist but her love of nursing could not be tempered. By the time that our paths were to become inextricably crossed they had been married for several years and were deeply engrossed in their respective careers. That is to say, they had no children.

Years later I would be told that these four remarkable people, my heroes to be, had sat at Sunday dinner and contemplated not their future, but mine. It just so happened that this was the day after Mom's attempted suicide. Mrs. Campbell had been keenly watching from a distance as her best friend's life gradually fell apart. Friends can do only so much, and then only what we allow them to do to help us. Joy made every attempt to be the good friend; however, she also realized that Gloria, my mom, had to help herself first before she could ever ask for help from friends. The foiled suicide attempt screamed that Mom needed help. Even more than her concern for her friend, Joy Campbell was concerned for me.

There can be no doubt in my mind that the discussion at dinner that Sunday was somber and heavy. Joy and Charles had already raised one child and were now middle-aged. Chuck and Karen were in their late 20s, had no child rearing experience, and were deeply career minded. Furthermore, there was the issue of no blood relationship to me whatsoever. That alone would have made for an easy way out. Yet these were people of conscience and conviction. They saw the opportunity to help a friend and just maybe help turn a kid around in the process. Had they done nothing, no one would have blamed them — no one, except themselves. The risks and sacrifices, certainly at the start, must have outweighed any possible promise. You see, I was well on my way to being a problem child.

Years of lacking strong parental guidance and a strong family home had left its toll. The interest in my dark side was beginning to rise. Associating, or attempting to associate, with older kids more interested in malice and mischief had already begun. My attitude and nature were increasingly surly. Interest in school was poor as my mediocre grades proved. Faculty members at St. John Berchman's, especially principal Sr. Elizabeth Marie, were confident that a more stable home life was the remedy for my poor academic showing. They felt that my talents and abilities were distracted and virtually untapped.

This is, I suppose, a perfect example of what was referred to in the late 20th century, as "the power of the village." Unrelated multiple influences with a remarkably similar approach and objective to developing a good citizen, and thereby a good society.

For me it is just one of an endless number of examples of how many people have blessed my life. Therefore, no adversity in my life could ever conquer the intricate web of love and compassion I have been blessed to know.

The decision was made. Despite the hardships and inconveniences that would undoubtedly have to be endured while undertaking this colossal effort, the Campbell's decided that the alternative was unacceptable. In their minds to turn their backs would be unforgivable.

What about Gloria? I cannot even begin to fathom what must have gone through my mom's mind when the idea was first suggested. No doubt she thought long and hard about it. Hindsight would also suggest that she was deeply alone considering the plan laid before her. The concern over her parents' influence prohibited that avenue of trust. Joy Campbell was her only real friend in sight, and there certainly didn't appear to be any additional family member capable, willing, or prepared to take in a troublesome 10-year-old boy. It must be understood that the events that transpired were done only with Mom's blessing and carried out only as she desired. There was no dark and seedy plan to steal me away from my family. The Campbells were not malicious or conniving in their efforts to offer me a better life and my mother a less troubled heart. Considering all the facts, what possible advantage could they have sought other than a simple act of goodwill and charity? These things must be said for over the years some people have suggested otherwise. For me to allow even the slightest suggestion that such an idea was possible would be criminal.

Shortly after Mom's "accident," Mrs. Campbell and her son Chuck showed up at our Canal Street home. My memory still finds that afternoon as odd and awkward for all parties concerned. There were just the four of us; no Nanny, no Grandpa, no Caru — just us. Even so I thought I was going to Mrs. Campbell's for the weekend. I do remember having spoken with her on the phone and crying earlier that day about how awful things had become at home. That experience, over the last several weeks, had become commonplace. Granted, the weekend away had been arranged rather hastily, but I was overjoyed at the chance to get away and have some fun. There was a tearful hug and kiss with Mom. Some two blocks later, while driving away in Chuck's truck, I asked Mrs. Campbell when I was coming back. As I turned my head to see my house fade in the distance, she replied "I don't know. For now you're going to have a new home with Chuck and his wife Karen. How does that sound?" At that moment my only concern was Mom. I asked "what about Mom?" Mrs. Campbell then explained that my mom had wanted it this way and that she would be okay. To say the least, I was sad and confused, wondering if I had been so bad that my mother didn't want me anymore. Mrs. Campbell reassured me that I had done nothing wrong and that this was for my own good.

Chuck and Karen lived in a really nice white house on Dudley Street, with black trim and two Grecian columns. It was as close to a mansion as I had ever seen – it wasn't one of course. They lived in the section of Shreveport known as South Highlands which was as nice as a young successful couple could find. It must be understood that I was not poor and the Campbells were not rich. It was just a completely different way of life and an appreciation for the alternatives in what life had to offer.

Karen greeted me warmly and affectionately upon my arrival. Yet I was still overwhelmed with sadness and confusion. In so many ways this wasn't home. How could it be? These were strangers. Friends yes, but strangers all the same. "My room" wasn't my room. It had none of my things and held no semblance of familiarity. There were so many nice things I was afraid to touch anything. "What if I broke something, would they send me back?" At age 10, considering the recent tempest of events in my life, there is no wonder I was slightly afraid. The true consolation was in their eyes. Chuck and Karen cared. Their eyes offered so much warmth and compassion it was impossible not to feel being loved. Even the menagerie of animals, two dogs and two cats, emphasized that these people were okay and I would be too. Besides, if Ms. Campbell brought me here, it had to be all right.

From the start it was clear that things were going to be very different. I was allowed a few days to settle in. After that, however, rules began to emerge that signaled my life was going to change – I for the better, even though I didn't care to see it that way. The times I spent with Joy Campbell could be unpleasant for me – she didn't put up with my "crap." She was always in control and left little room for me to behave like the spoiled brat I had become. Life with Chuck and Karen would be much the same way.

Chuck was even more of a stern taskmaster than his mom. Not like my grandfather had been, but in a loving way. The Campbells had thought long and hard about the proper course of action required to tame me. Joy had made it abundantly clear to my mom that what I needed was a firm hand and not a blind eye. Over the years I would discover that Chuck was absolutely perfect for this role, for he had been an unruly child himself. Like Chuck's mom, Karen's mom (Mrs. Bolte, or "Mrs. B.") was also a no nonsense kind of mother, though in a different way. Regardless, Karen appreciated the importance of discipline while understanding the need for love and nurturing. Between the two of them I would, in time, transform into a well behaved young gentleman.

There were certain character flaws in desperate need of immediate attention and the Campbells were determined to address them. Seemingly unimportant to me, my lack of courtesy and basic manners was the first to be rectified. As shall be recalled, my hatred of vegetables was infamous. It seems natural that the dinner table was an excellent place to begin my transformation. Chuck loved peas and carrots, mixed. What a horror! It was made perfectly clear that I had certain responsibilities while living under Chuck and Karen's roof. Regarding meals, I was to help set and clear the table as well as eat everything on my plate. It wasn't a problem, until we came to foods I didn't like, or *thought* I didn't like. Karen's dad, Mr. B, was an amateur gourmet chef and had instilled in his children the importance of trying many different kinds of food. Mrs. B, a depression child, had drilled the importance of "waste not, want not." Therefore, backed by Chuck's fatherly demeanor, Karen set about the long arduous task of teaching me proper table etiquette. In addition to learning proper table setting protocol, I was not allowed to leave the table without cleaning my plate. Until this point I had been able to eat what I wanted at the risk of throwing a temper tantrum. In this household, that did not work! There was many a night I was forced to wait at the table until I had struggled with swallowing the peas, *or* broccoli, *or* even worse – the dreaded lima beans. In the end my eating habits and table manners were transformed from nonexistent, to socially graceful. Granted it took two or three years, but that is compared to 10 years of being a spoiled brat.

The dinner table was only the beginning. There was an entire character to remold. My cosmetic appearance was in dire need of attention. My hair was in need of professional grooming; my fingernails were never clean; I hated to brush my teeth; I had no idea what was meant by "proper attire". Even normal toiletry practices had to be stressed and taught. It should not be interpreted that I had been raised improperly. On the contrary, rather these were all normal habits that had fallen by the wayside in the wake of a seriously disrupted home life. God bless Chuck and Karen for their intestinal fortitude.

It must have taken saintly patience and love to endure the daily task of remolding a child, not from birth, but already 10 years grown. It is no wonder that, after me, Chuck and Karen had no children of their own.

Life with the Campbell's exposed me to a larger world of culture and expanded my horizons. Both households contained an endless collection of antiques and fine furnishings. From Persian rugs to fine china and crystal, as well as a varied selection of American and English antique furniture, the Campbells sought to surround themselves with some of life's luxuries. Yet despite these trappings, there was no evidence of haughtiness or arrogance. On the contrary my new guardians simply had an appreciation for class and quality. They stressed that no possessions or amount of materialism could assure one of class. That personal attribute was a result of love and careful child rearing. One could have all the wealth and luxury in the world, but what mattered most was the appreciation of the character and intrinsic value those possessions held. The history behind them and the craftsmanship of their creation was of more importance than their market value. It was here that I began to understand a key precept of my life; there is no monetary or material equivalent to an individual's principles.

Having come from a musical family, similar to the Von Trapps from *The Sound of Music*, Karen knew how important musical training could be. In addition to instilling discipline and fostering a love for music, such lessons would undoubtedly assist my efforts to become a better student. It was initially decided that I should begin studying the piano. There were many fond childhood memories of sitting at the piano with my mom, so naturally that was the instrument for me. Eddie Kozak, a local private teacher, became my tutor. There were weekly lessons and at least one hour of practice per day. It would be over four years before two facts would become undeniably clear. First, I didn't have much natural talent for the instrument. Second, to become a Van Clyburn, one must practice! Nonetheless, that experience set in motion a lifelong pursuit of bringing more music into the world. My talents may not have been musically artistic, but I would soon discover that the world of music needs patrons almost as much as it needs musicians.

At age nine Karen introduced me to the Shreveport Summer Music Festival. My association with that organization would last fourteen years and lead me into a fraternal bonding that will continue until I die.

Chuck also decided that I would overcome my "Sissy" reputation in the traditionally American way — through sports. He was convinced that combined with a strong male influence, previously lacking in my life, participation in team sports would toughen me up. Having suffered some serious knee injuries from high school football himself, Chuck suggested perhaps basketball and baseball. I loved baseball while hating basketball. Regardless, as long as grades didn't suffer, my fate was sealed – like it or not, I would play. Prior to Chuck's influence there had been no one to show me the basics of physical coordination. Furthermore, I can recall absolutely not one person in my life that showed an interest in sports. Consequently, I was no jock and physically lacked the adolescent preparation most boys obtain from family or friends. In hindsight, if there had been a soccer program, considering my love of kickball, I might have been decent at that. As it was, after two years of baseball and basketball I could claim no trophies or metals. However, the experience improved me physically, from chubby to thin, and my hand to eye coordination did develop. More importantly my efforts, though feeble at best, dramatically altered my standing with the other guys in my class. For the first time my status changed from being a sissy to being just a brainy wimp.

Chuck and Karen's greatest influence was to instill a love of reading and education. They taught me *to love to learn, not love to earn*! Having been a poor student himself, Chuck told me that he would never allow any of his children to suffer the same mistakes. So it began. On each school night, after dinner, I could be found encamped at my desk. Chuck taught me how to become more organized with my time and my study aids. Early on it was stressed that I had a personal responsibility to myself regarding unfamiliar words and their meanings. No one was going to just give me the definition of a word. If I didn't know it, then I'd have to look it up in the dictionary. Chuck and Karen made sure that a dictionary, thesaurus, and atlas were readily accessible – permanent resources at my desk. They emphasized their willingness to help with problems I was unable to figure out for myself, *but I had to honestly try first.* There was a notebook for each subject and one to record daily assignments. To some this all may seem tedious, yet for me it worked.

To instill a love of reading, my TV time was restricted and I was given a slew of books to be read. There were American classics such as James Fennimore Cooper's *The Leather Stocking Tales*, Shakespeare's plays, several of Jules Verne's novels, and a library of others in addition to the reading lists I had from school. Chuck and Karen insisted that as long as I had books to read, there was no excuse for me to have nothing to do. All of these guidelines were designed to assist me in becoming a better student and actually enjoy learning. They knew I had the brain, if only I was properly trained on how to use it. In addition the Campbells distinguished the difference between facts and knowledge, and how to apply it. For the first time I was taught the value of cognitive reasoning and logical thinking. Over the years this cornerstone of learning, enhanced by formal education, would prove invaluable.

As case and point, within two years – from sixth to eighth grades – my academic progress soared. I went from C's and D's to A's and B's, graduating second in my elementary school class. The awards on graduation night were so numerous for my outstanding improvement that I had to use my hardcover diploma as a tray. Without my mom's sacrifice, the Campbell's patience, determination, *and most of all – their love* none of it would have ever been possible.

Graduation day was filled with excitement. I had no idea how personally successful it would be. Yet the mere fact of graduating and moving on to high school was enough for me. In addition Mom and my biological grandparents would be present. It thrilled me to know that they would be there to see the actual result of so much hard work. I had no idea that the evening would be the beginning of a rift to last for many years.

After the actual ceremony and awards presentation, there was a reception in the school gymnasium. The Campbell's, the Riley's, Caru and her husband Austin, my mom and I all gathered together for the first time since I had come to live with Chuck and Karen, two years earlier. There had been visits back to see Mom for holidays as well as a few gatherings with some of my other biological relatives. However, the actual contact with my "real" grandparents had been limited at best. I was not privy to the actual conversation between the Campbell's and the Riley's that evening. It was my night and standing in the corner with the grown-ups was not my first priority. My time was spent mostly with Mom. It wasn't until arriving home later on Dudley Street that I learned of the evenings behind the scene events.

Karen and Charles, and especially Chuck and Joy, were incensed at my grandparents. Apparently, the Riley's implied that the Campbell's had turned me into a snob and showed absolutely no gratitude for the remarkable job they had done. The Riley's displeasure probably masked their feelings of guilt and inadequacy. The concern was raised that perhaps it was time for me to return to the family fold. Nanny and Grandpa stressed that since Caru was on her own it was now possible for them to care for me. Ironically, according to the Campbell's, this sudden surge of interest arose just after I began receiving Social Security dependent income; my biological father, Tommy Sr., had recently passed away, initiating this recent increase in personal income.

I remember Caru, as well as my grandparents, actually beaming with pride for me that evening. As the reception began to draw to a close I remember my mom being very sad and distraught. My impression had been that she was merely saddened at our parting again. She had noted tearfully that she was just so proud of me but also extremely tired; it had been a long day for her. Later Mrs. Campbell, Joy, explained my grandparents had been rude and insulting, suggesting that the Campbell's were trying to keep me away from my biological family. To this day I still do not know what happened, except what I was told. Again, like so many arguments, the facts have been lost as the parties have passed on. It doesn't really matter. What does matter is that it would be years before ill feelings would ever be partially healed, and then only after a loved one died. What I do know is that my mom had been quite clear that she would rather I live with Chuck and Karen, under the close eye of her best friend, Joy Campbell, than for me to return to the Canal Street or Lakehurst residences. If nothing else, that graduation night proved the Campbells were on the right track.

Throughout one's life people come and go. Friends, family, colleagues, acquaintances, etc…all leave a mark on the character of our lives. Some are positive; some are negative; few are life changing, and even fewer are monumental. Each interacts with us either by choice or circumstance. Those interactions, regardless of frequency or depth of involvement, each leave some degree of influence. Wisdom after many years of living and interacting with others teaches us that we are rarely disappointed in people themselves, but rather in our mistaken expectations of how we want them to be. My biological grandparents and my sister weren't bad people, they just didn't behave in the manner I had hoped and prayed for, over the years of our relationship. I'm sure as well they felt the same about me.

6

ABUSIVE, GUTLESS, OR IN DENIAL

ABUSE BETRAYS CHARACTER ... For years I have purposely avoided discussing a very controversial subject in my past due to the potential harm and cascading repercussions it could cause to individuals still very dear to me. In contemporary times the origins of one's "sexual orientation" has transformed into a debate over whether one is born a particular way or were they merely influenced into a way of life by circumstances and/or other individuals. My personal case, in my opinion, transcends this controversy because depending on your point of view my sexual orientation fits both.

While writing about these experiences in my life, certain recent events (in our contemporary society) have developed that give me pause. Numerous situations involving sexual harassment, child abuse, and allegations of improper behavior have focused the public's attention on these issues. In each case legal repercussions and claims of character assassination have resulted in the irreversible changing of lives. For these reasons and these reasons alone I believe circumstances in my past are somewhat relevant. However, revelation of my personal experiences should in no way be interpreted as an attempt to profit for personal or financial gain from the tragic news of the day. Rather, my hope is to take this moment and explain how similar events in my life developed and attempt to demonstrate that perceived adversity *CAN* build character.

From the outset I want to be perfectly clear that despite the details being revealed, I in no way hold any individual responsible for the result. On the contrary: I am a firm believer that we are who we are from birth as a natural fact, and while life experiences may influence our decisions, it is our true nature that matures into being. Granted undue influence from coercion, guilt or necessity exert an overwhelming degree of pressure in the end result; it is our freedom of choice and how we cope with those choices that are the primary indicator of who we are. In other words when confronted with an either/or decision, one still has the ultimate freedom of choice as to which way you go. For most, the determining factors involve a cost/benefit analysis or perhaps an appraisal of the potential versus the probable risks. Regardless, the final choice one makes is a pretty good indicator of a person's core values.

While an individual, in most cases, has the final say so as to the choices he or she makes there is one mitigating criteria that society and the law consider so overreaching that it supersedes normal circumstances: age. In other words we as human beings do not reach a level of maturity and emotional competence to warrant complete cognizance of the repercussions of our actions or those actions inflicted upon us. Therefore, both the law and society hold adults accountable on a higher standard for their interactions with children or "minors." *This is how it should be*; for as children we are brought up to respect our elders and believe that they should know better. This conscious distinction of knowing right from wrong is especially true in the realm of sexual relations. When combined with the overwhelming influence inflicted upon a child because of the moray of respect, not to mention a physiological superiority in strength and physical size, a child or "minor" is generally at a distinct disadvantage to resist or rebuke the will of an adult. These lines of demarcation are becoming more and more blurred than in the past because of the influence of the "information age." "Young people" today know more about sex than a generation ago. The influence of modern media and technology have made this a given. However, "lines in the sand" must still be drawn as to what is acceptable and what is not to be tolerated between children and adults. I attempt to make these distinctions because while I was not physically "abused" or psychologically impaired from my personal experience, my case is an exception to the rule – in my personal opinion.

As is so often the case in our society the subject eventually comes up when you are asked, "How did it start?" or "When did you first do IT?" or, please forgive the more vulgar description, "When did you lose your cherry?" Nonetheless, our "first time" stands out in our lives as a transformational experience. Mine is no different. Due to the fact that certain individuals are still living and the revered memories of others still linger, I shall refrain from naming names or making prejudicial accusations that could very well damage or seriously jeopardize the happy lives of people I still care a great deal about. In fact the only reason I even decided to reveal these events is because they *DID* happen in my life and while many might describe them as an adversity, I do not. The truth, as I see it, is that my first sexual experiences, regardless of the moral or legal perceptions, were simply a verification of my true nature as I was born to be. Individuals can make their own decisions regarding the events and the participants, but as far as I am concerned, I was not abused and the events were of mutual, though perhaps naïve, consent. As I look back, it all seems to begin when I was but still a young boy, for that is my first memory and confused recollection regarding sexual arousal. The event happened innocently enough in the school library when the recent copy of the Sports Illustrated "Swimsuit" edition was suddenly thrust in front of me by a classmate who exclaimed, "Here Ufert. See if this does anything for ya!" Over the next several minutes I timidly thumbed through the endless pages of scantily clad swimsuit models displayed so erotically for my young eyes to feast upon. As I turned one particular page there suddenly was a Jockey underwear ad with Baltimore Orioles pitching great Jim Palmer wearing only a sexy pair of bikini briefs. It hit me like a lightning bolt to my confused, astonished, and ashamed young mind. Unlike the numerous pages of beautiful and sexy female swimsuit models, this single picture was instantaneously arousing. Though I very quickly turned to the following pages with disguised embarrassment, it left a lifelong impression.

For years I had struggled to personally deny and publicly refute every accusation of homosexual tendencies. Yet in that single moment my worst fear glared back at me like a crowd of finger pointing accusatorial clergy during the era of the Spanish Inquisition. Simultaneously it was both embarrassing and humiliating to acknowledge my deepest fears of being physically aroused at the site of a scantily clad muscular man.

Yet the reaction was instantaneous, spontaneous, and uncontrollable. In hindsight I can now point to this one instant as the undeniable confirmation that I am gay, and always have been. However, it would take many years of frustration, curiosity, experimentation, and denial before I could honestly accept who I am. Furthermore, due to my feverish attempts to accomplish social, academic, and professional notoriety – endless efforts to rationalize, excuse, and ignore my true feelings would "keep me in the closet."

My first admission of these feelings was made innocently and timidly to a trusted and revered mentor. The subject came up innocently enough, during a rather nonchalant private conversation between the two of us regarding "the birds and the bees." This trusted family friend asked rather casually, "what exactly in the magazine turned you on?" I should explain that even though contemporary society does not "talk about it," it is rather common for discussions to occur between younger and older males about sex as a form of discrete & innocent means to provide very important, and in today's world, even life-saving, sex education. Therefore, this older family friend's somewhat embarrassing question was not exactly anything to be considered unusual or inappropriate. In fact even now, as I did then, my opinion is still that this was simply part of the normal process in seeking advice about an embarrassing subject between a somewhat naïve younger boy and an older, mature, and certainly more experienced trusted male friend. Granted, in most cases these discussions occur between fathers and sons. However in today's society where the family unit has dramatically changed, it is more common than not, that such talks *DO* occur between men and boys who are not necessarily related as father and son.

For this reason I encourage others not to make any quick judgments based on traditionally held prejudices. I certainly do not, nor did I then. This initial encounter, in most opinions, would be considered completely within the norm and undeniably appropriate. As the story unfolds however, there can be no doubt that any degree of acceptance and appropriateness will dramatically shift.

Rather timidly, I confessed to my embarrassment that I became immediately aroused at the image of that famous ballplayer's obvious sexual "package" enticingly displayed in the underwear ad. Without any expression of embarrassment or prejudice my "mentor" inquired further as to why I thought this particular photograph was more arousing than any other. Without going into any unnecessary graphic detail I shall simply say that the discussion continued for some time and ended, as I recall, with a simple pat on the back and my older trusted friend dismissing the event simply by saying "I wouldn't worry about it 'Sport,' things like that happen to all us guys as we're growing up. It's kind of a competitive thing; every guy wants to be bigger and better than the next." With that our first man-to-man talk ended, leaving me with the impression that there was nothing weird or unnatural about it at all. In fact the entire experience made me feel more comfortable and reassured than I had before, and certainly far less embarrassed. For that alone I was deeply grateful.

It would be several weeks before an additional man-to-man talk was to occur. It should be noted that none of the encounters between me and my "mentor" were ever scheduled or really planned; they just seemed to happen whenever time or scheduling permitted. The obvious age difference between us and the fact that my "mentor" was a married man complicated our situation, but in some ways seemed to be mutually beneficial. In the beginning our "talks" primarily focused on the typical physical, emotional and biological changes happening to me, as they do to all boys reaching puberty. My "mentor" was always friendly, attentive, and demonstrated genuine concern for my feelings and how these changes affected me. Over the years I have learned that this is a rather typical approach for the stereotypical pedophile. Regardless of the legal and social definition, even today I do not really consider my former family friend to have been your typical pedophile. Yes, he was an adult and I was a child. However, I have no evidence that suggests he has ever behaved similarly before or since. I am not foolish enough to believe that it is not possible, but knowing this individual as well as I do, pedophilia tendencies were never detected in his character. It is my firm belief that in my case it was simply a matter of convenience that he took advantage of me and that I was obviously complicit in our actions.

Speaking of actions, there should be little doubt that our "talks" gradually progressed into physical contact. In hindsight, "with age comes wisdom," I must admit my naïveté is somewhat humorous. I don't make jest or in any way attempt to trivialize the rather despicable and outrageous acts of pedophilia, but rather denote how unbelievably obvious his "act" seems to me now. The groundwork for our first physical encounter was laid a couple of weeks earlier, before one of our "talks." Furthermore, the entire setting was craftily camouflaged in an air of genuine concern for my health and physical well-being. At that particular time in my life I was genuinely concerned and deeply embarrassed about the natural pubescent experience of "wet dreams." Voicing my concerns naturally led to a rather detailed and esoteric explanation of why pubescent males experience this phenomenon. This in turn led to the inevitable inquiry as to my knowledge of and routine method of ejaculation or orgasm. To say the least, despite the several months of increased comfort and relaxation with our discussions about sex, I was naturally highly embarrassed and timid to ever admit to anyone – especially an adult – about ever masturbating. To alleviate any fears of long – held Catholic guilt, my "mentor" simply noted that "everybody does it" and there was nothing to worry about. Being inexperienced, I described the only way I knew how "to get off." At this point he asked if I would mind demonstrating what I meant because he feigned a lack of comprehension after my description. Though somewhat unsure, but being in a natural state of physical arousal from our discussion, I agreed. For the next few minutes he simply sat and watched as I lay on the floor and "humped" till I relieved myself. The entire experience occurred while we were both fully clothed. This set the stage for my first sexual experience with another human being.

While alone together for a holiday weekend in a secluded setting of rest, relaxation, and male to male bonding, the two of us lounged around, watched TV, and generally "hung out." During dinner we watched a prime time baseball game followed by an episode of Charlie's Angels. Generally my "mentor" relaxed wearing only a T-shirt, his BVDs, and socks. No big deal, it was just us guys. The next day's plan called for an early start to the day so we called it a night and prepared for bed. This particular weekend our accommodations were limited to a single large bed for the both of us. Having worked a tough schedule all week, and planning to arise early in the morning he climbed into bed first and asked me to turn off the light after I undressed but before I lay down. I did so but was a bit shy and tried to hide my obvious erection within my briefs. For the next several minutes I tossed and turned unable to fall asleep. At this point he very calmly explained that neither of us was going to be able to get any sleep until "I took care of my problem." He then commented how he usually had problems getting to sleep when aroused. After a long pause my "mentor," in a very fatherly tone, expressed some concern he had been having since our last talk; namely that the method of masturbation I had demonstrated at that time might result in an infection caused from abrasion. He offered, if I was willing, to show me the way he and most other guys "did it." That night I saw my first naked man, had my first homosexual contact, and experienced my first mutual "hand job."

Over the next several months this encounter would be repeated numerous times and gradually advance to additional levels of homosexuality as well as provide easy access to "straight" pornography. Throughout this period of increased activity, our experiences were continuously rationalized as "buddies helping each other out." Furthermore, it was stressed from the very beginning that every aspect of our encounters must be kept absolutely secret from everybody – *no one must know* – "they would not understand and *we* could get into trouble." It was never discussed in any detail what he meant by "trouble." In my mind I thought he just meant others would not approve – it never occurred to me that there were very serious legal repercussions for him should our "little secret" ever be discovered. In addition I had no concept of the catastrophic moral implications involved with what might well be considered "abusive" behavior. These encounters continued for a period of 2 to 3 years. Gradually over that time it became increasingly evident to me that I honestly enjoyed our experiences and even eagerly anticipated them. There were times when my libido was so overpowering that I actually encouraged and plotted situations to ensure sexual contact. Some might say that these were merely the expected consequences of an immature and over stimulated pubescent young boy. In some ways they would be right. However, only blind stupidity would allow a reasonable mind not to conclude that this was a clear case of an adult taking advantage of a child's probable sexual orientation for his own personal benefit. Whatever his personal reasons, I no longer care. During our last sexual encounter, my encouragement and "attempts to please" my sexual "mentor," as demonstrated by my unmistakable "body language," were rebuked and instantly rejected. At the time I was dismayed and humiliated, only to realize years later this was simply his stern acknowledgment that things had gone too far. He and I have never spoken of these encounters since. My only regret is that his personal and private denials of the true nature of the events that transpired prevented him from providing me the loving and supportive counseling that could have been extremely helpful to me throughout my teenage years. His lack of courage and honesty resulted in years of denial and shame for me personally that may very well have set in motion sexual behavior in my past that could easily be described as dangerous and destructive. Furthermore, my denial and shame reached such extreme levels that I even rebuked and castigated others in an attempt to shift attention from myself and futilely disguise my own guilt. Here and now I deeply and wholeheartedly apologize to any and all individuals that I had ever publicly or privately criticized, condemned, or ridiculed for being gay.

Furthermore, I do not condone in any way the sexual abuse of any individual – especially children or minors. Sexual interaction with anyone against their will is unconscionable and persons who use their positions of authority or influence, in any situation, to coerce another into having sex are wrong. Such activity leaves an indelible mark upon the victim that can never be erased or forgotten. For many individuals, sexual abuse mars them for life and for this reason it is imperative that society recognizes the debilitating results of such abuse. A recent public service campaign coined the phrase "it does get better!" *I am living proof that it does indeed get better.* I encourage victims of sexual abuse to speak out, take a stand, and show the world that abuse will not conquer their character or define their lives.

Finally I wish to deeply stress that many details and extensive descriptions of these events in my life have been purposefully omitted to avoid detracting from the overall intention of this work, i.e., to inspire.

Shortly after this terrible ordeal I spent an entire summer with Karen's family in Erie, Pennsylvania. That summer would help me deal with my confused feelings and give me a renewed sense of confidence. Karen's parents, Ruth and Frank Bolte, lived in a spacious farmhouse in Fairview, just outside of Erie. Mr. and Mrs. "B" were remarkable people. Their home, though graciously furnished and situated on several acres of rural countryside, contained innumerable collections of stunning grandfather clocks, antiques, and invaluable memorabilia collected over the years. Mr. B. spent his time as a well-respected building contractor performing numerous tasks for several private clients. He was a rather tall jovial fellow of German descent who was a renowned bass trombonist. In fact all of Karen's family members were very accomplished musicians: her brother Fred, like his father was a bass trombonist; her mom (Mrs. B.) played piano, clarinet, and organ; her sister Liz was a bassoonist, while Karen was a violist. This musical family history played a major role in developing my love for music and lifelong desire to support the arts.

While visiting the Boltes that summer I was blessed to discover my *Happy Place*. Located directly behind their farmhouse, about a thousand yards away, was a small wild cherry orchard and wooded area. A small babbling brook had originally meandered through the middle of this lush forested patch of land. However, over the years wild beavers had damned the brook causing a serene peaceful pond to develop. This Walden-like atmosphere was the ideal place for a young man to recline on a boat while fishing, and lazily gander at the bright blue sky and endless billowing snow white clouds. Literally speaking, this piece of heaven on earth gave me peace and solitude to cherish for the rest of my life. Even today, just like the summer after my soul-torturing fiasco with "my mentor", picturesque memories of my *happy place* transport me to a peaceful realm of tranquility and solitude that cannot be conquered by stress or despair. When times are troubling and hope seems forever lost, there lies such a place in each of our hearts that no darkness shall ever conquer! Only through gut wrenching and life altering adversity did I learn to cherish and forever hold dear that memory of a carefree time when happiness seemed eternal. Each of us must preserve our *happy places* with an unbreakable bond as if our lives depended on it — the time will come when that may very well be true! Memories of happier times and places keep us sane and re-assured that hope is not lost in the face of our adversity.

7

PAWN WHO WOULD BE KING

THE SPLENDOR OF my elementary graduation was short-lived. Starting Jesuit high school meant that once again I was a small fish in a bigger pond, as is usually the case. The transformation from grade school to high school normally is a major adjustment. Attending Jesuit, a small private all male Catholic prep-school meant an even higher degree of competition. Regarded as one of the finest secondary institutions in Louisiana, the school had a reputation of "weeding" out the men from the boys. Chuck himself had attended in the 60s and his stories only added more apprehension. Boys from all over the region competed for placement. Since the student body numbered less than 500, attendees were considered the best of the best.

Life at Jesuit begins the spring prior to your first year with the school's orientation night for prospective students and their parents. As is typical, such a gathering is well organized and designed to anticipate all potential issues raised by parents and students alike. Representatives from the school in the fields of academics, athletics, extracurricular activities, spiritual and character development, college bound preparation, and infrastructure details were all present to offer a comprehensive overview of a Jesuit education. Regarded as the finest private school instruction in the area, Jesuit High School, formally known as St. John's College Prep, had the reputation for being academically challenging, athletically motivating, and socially unsurpassed. It fit as closely as possible to the private boarding school role model, without the boarding part, that could be achieved. Even its brochure picture invoked a sense of history and respect displaying the main red brick building in black & white celluloid as if to say, "send you sons here and they're destined to conquer first Harvard, and then the world." No denying that the school's public reputation was certainly supported by the historical fact of having educated many of the community's social and financial elite, generation after generation. Though small, this institution was regarded for decades as the bastion of the best education money could buy.

After the initial presentation for students and parents combined, the two groups were then separated into a private orientation for each. This was designed to give both parties a chance to meet and bond with their respective peer group and address relevant issues. Considering the community-wide draw from numerous public and parochial grammar schools, Jesuit educated a melting pot of students from diverse social, academic, and economic backgrounds. This evening would be the beginning of a four year adventure that would in most cases lead to friendships and relationships lasting a lifetime. Such a foundation for life-long development of character and relations can be the success and or failure of one's private and public life. In hind sight such gatherings have been the cornerstone of people's lives; hence, the unparalleled importance of one's first impressions – rightly or wrongly – they can last a lifetime. We each know all too well the particular atmosphere of evaluation and categorization that pervades every initial gathering of people. It is *our nature* to "size up" our potential friends and enemies.

We only learn later in life that you "can't judge a book by its cover." Real life experience teaches us those personal attributes we come to appreciate and those we despise in others. However, the social interaction at school is the training ground for our lives to come. For this reason, numerous sociological studies verify that the playground and the classroom are the incubators of our relations to the world and people around us. This night was no different.

Some thirty years later, I can look back and point to individuals that left lasting impressions both mentally and physically in my mind. Those first impressions would affect how I perceived others and my relationship to them – some correctly, but many surprisingly would transform over the years. Some of those same people I had attended grammar school with, but most were new faces unknown to me. Those I knew from grade school had seen the beginning stages of my transformation and were either impressed or ambivalent. The new guys did not know me, my history, or my previous accomplishments and vice versa.

At one time I described the transition from grade school to high school, and then to college, as a big fish suddenly being transported from a small pond into a lake and then again into an ocean. The surrounding environment is similar and all the creatures seem to be the same. Yet over time, in some cases a very short amount of time, reality comes into focus and you realize you are not as big a fish as you thought. In fact, it becomes very clear you are a minnow surrounded by sharks and barracudas. You either adapt to survive or accept to be eaten. That's life. School is just a microcosm of society as a whole; the larger the school – the more public the school, the smaller the luxuries are and therefore the more intense the competition for limited resources. Yet a larger environment with a more diverse population provides endless opportunities to grow, learn, and improve. This is where you either sink or swim. The point is, throughout life we take those early lessons from our educational environment with us. It's that simple.

*   *   *   *

"Check Mate!" Who would have thought that those two little words would come to be a positive mark of distinction for a four year academic and social rebirth? That is just what happened. Nerdy and socially "pariah-like", chess playing became my claim to fame in high school. Chess was the foundation of my notoriety. The game challenged my mind, organized my thought processes, and as you might expect, garnered a reputation throughout Jesuit High School. Granted, the initial distinction was not a desired one. It is not difficult to imagine the typical stereotype one pictures of a young man actively involved in the daily participation of playing chess especially in an all male high school setting. From the beginning, there were the expected jeers and puns heaped upon me from the "jocks." The "cool" upperclassman made a daily point of reminding me how such behavior was viewed. To the average observer, chess is considered an "intellectual" pursuit sought by only the socially and "physically challenged;" you know, nerds, fags, brainiacs, and wimps. It is certainly not known as a stepping stone to a higher and more desirable social status in the high school world. Yet by some weird twist of fate and an innumerable list of coincidences, that is exactly what transpired. A seemingly queer, brainy, nerd rose like a phoenix from the ashes of social obscurity to the greatest heights of the typical high school social hierarchy. One would think, coupled with my past history from St. John's, that playing chess would only add to my status as a social outcast. I had two things going for me…one, my newfound sense of self-importance, confidence and respect gained from my academic accomplishments in grade school; and second, development of a new desire to be more socially accepted by my peers. On the surface both of these trends seemed positive, however without proper guidance, support, and direction, they can be equally destructive. Thanks to some genuine love and ardent character building from the Campbells, initial pitfalls were avoided.

Jesuit was a wonderful place to grow, learn, and improve. Over the next four years, that is just what I would do. Playing chess helped me grow, learn, and improve.

The differences between Jesuit High School and St. John's grade school were dramatic and immediate; that was apparent at the freshman orientation conducted in the early summer after eighth grade. After graduating second in my class from St. John's, I came to high school with a chip on my shoulder, rather impressed with myself. That feeling quickly crashed and burned on the first day of orientation. Our principal Mr. Ernst erased every study method we had ever been taught. He said, "Forget what you think you know about studying. Here it doesn't apply!" We were instructed for three days in the "SQ3R" methodology of studying. I must admit, it has stuck with me ever since. According to the basic tenets of this theory, a student must learn and forget; learn and forget; *learn to retain.* This is in striking contrast to memorizing and forgetting. With one, you learn it – it becomes part of you. With the other, you memorize it to pass a single exam. After that, you forget it. This methodology stressed abbreviated note taking, associative learning, deductive reasoning, and logical analysis: Classical education. One yearned to learn, rather than, yearned to earn! Perhaps some of my fellow students gained a different perspective from this educational training and would disagree with my conclusions. So be it! This is my story, they can write their own.

In many ways, an outsider might observe the atmosphere at Jesuit, as did F. Scott Fitzgerald writing about East and West Egg in *The Great Gatsby.* Granted, this was a world of privilege because it was private education where the more affluent sent their sons, yet the socialization process is not unlike that of any other high school. In my opinion, the faculty and the curriculum strove to bring out the highest traits in each boy to prepare them for the expected rigors of their future college bound careers. There were times later in my extracurricular experiences, because of my limited economic means, that some of my classmates reminded me of the "Tom & Daisy Buchanan's" described so eloquently by Fitzgerald. However, by the time we graduated, I was "one of the boys in the club" even if I could not afford the social life they preferred.

Now a freshman, I was once again at the bottom of the ladder. There were upperclassmen who remembered me from earlier years at St. John's, so naturally, my previous reputation as a sissy/wimp followed me despite my miraculous accomplishments. To overcompensate, I was intent on excelling in my academic as well as extracurricular activities. Having performed poorly in elementary athletics, I chose to participate in other after school pursuits. Having been blessed with the gift of gab, my interest immediately focused on debate. It seemed ideally suited for my talents and career aspirations. Early on, I felt a desire to seek a future in law, to Chuck and Karen's dismay. The futility of such a goal had not yet sunk in. Law was the logical choice for any aspiring politically minded young man, despite industry statistics that demonstrated there were more law school students then successful attorneys. Yet I dove into debate with drive and passion. Coupled with my studies in Latin and history, the required research and organizational skills that debate demanded further enhanced my academic efforts.

The academic curriculum stressed an increasingly difficult level of knowledge and application, with emphasis on the "classics." Our freshman year began with English, Algebra I, Theology, IPS (Introductory Physical Science), Gym, American history, a foreign language, and Speech – none of these was intended to be a "breeze." With each passing year, our classwork would follow a similar, though dramatically more difficult structure and an increasingly intense degree of study. For example, each year we were required to study a Shakespearean play in English class. The depth and proficiency of our foreign language studies also intensified; in fact, we were encouraged to learn more than a single foreign language before graduation. I myself took Latin and German. In addition, our studies in mathematics, science and history became more deliberate and expansive in our depth of knowledge and understanding.

Ironically, my choices for extracurricular pastimes only added to the stereotype my peers had already confirmed upon me. Furthermore, debating's constant honing of my argument techniques turned almost every discussion into a verbal battle. This resulted in an overblown ego. Consequently, I began to alienate even my loved ones, not to mention my fellow classmates. Finally, in my sophomore year Chuck forced me to withdraw from debate. Thank God, because in later years I would see very well how such a trend can lead to complete isolation. Chess club would be my impetus to notoriety.

*   *   *   *

Caru showed up unexpected and unannounced during lunch break in the spring of my high school sophomore year. Rumors had already reached me through the grapevine that her four year marriage was in shambles. Husband, Austin, supposedly had returned to Vivian, Louisiana, and divorce proceedings were in process. We had not spoken since elementary graduation night. Frankly, I had no desire to see or speak with my sister now. After my feelings of abandonment because of Mom, I held little regard or respect for Caru. Furthermore, there was some degree of embarrassment that my friends and teachers would discover all the awful truths about our past family life. Ridiculous adolescent fears can be powerful incentives to hurt or ignore the ones we are supposed to love. I suppose that is part of human nature.

Approaching me initially in the cafeteria, I failed to recognize her. Remember it had been several years since our last meeting. Amid hoots and catcalls from my classmates whose libidos were obviously impressed with her striking good looks, I cautiously approached this "stranger." Once face-to-face, I knew it was Caru. Her presence immediately resurrected ill feelings that swept over me like a tidal wave. I brushed her off as one would an annoying insect and refused to speak with her. I left her crying and pleading for my fraternal affection. Unfortunately, my heart for Caru was neither cold nor stone; it simply was not there at all!

The short encounter had left me shaken and confused. The natural love for my only sibling was in sharp conflict with years of animosity that Caru could not really be held accountable for. Yet my pride refused to waiver in the face of compassion. She however was more determined, and that in and of itself demonstrated her love for me. After locating me in my next class, she courteously requested that my teacher allow us to speak. Under duress, I agreed. Teary-eyed and emotional she explained that she had enlisted in the Air Force and would be leaving the country the next day. She lovingly noted that all she wanted was to see me and ask for my blessing. Coldly, I flatly refused. I do not think I have ever regretted any single act more than that one. It certainly sealed our relationship for years to come. Perhaps, one of the many good things that this book will achieve is Carolyn's, "Caru's", forgiveness.

*   *   *   *

As I have noted late in grade school the game of chess became not just a pastime, but rather almost an obsession. There were so many classmates challenging me to a game that I was forced to keep a daily schedule and calendar of opponents. Chuck and Karen encouraged my interest for its obvious mental promise. Chess is a thinking game that requires forethought, planning, keen observation, and deep concentration. As I have also noted most of my classmates considered enthusiasts of the game to be… nerds; equivalent to computer geeks and Dungeons and Dragons aficionados. Well, so be it. Already considered weird and brainy, I figured why not.

Previously in the spring of our first year, I and another debate team member set about starting the Jesuit Chess Club. We went all out following school procedures for starting a new club, seeking members, and promoting our efforts. It was a grueling social endeavor because our classmates had labeled us as stereotypes. John and I were not concerned and just laughed off the insults. Fortunately, with administration support we made contact with other such clubs at neighboring schools. In fact, within two years our club had help to establish five others across the city, held weekly practice sessions, organized interclub matches, and hosted an annual citywide high school tournament with trophies. By my junior year, our fellow students could laugh and tease us with such comments as, "Hey, Ufert! Still weightlifting with those chess pieces?" But they could no longer afford to disregard us. Though the serious membership was a small core, the chess club grew to be the largest academic organization on campus and its treasury was one of the wealthiest. Granted our membership requirements were minimal – dues paying, a token expression of interest, *and breathing*. Furthermore, as people approached their senior year, memberships in extracurricular clubs were highly sought after for the sake of transcripts on college applications. It was a small price of indignity to pay for the school wide respect the chess club gained. In the end, it was the sole reason for my name recognition as I considered running for student body president.

Time had been devoted to my grades, chess club, and some minor extracurricular activities. Not until my junior year had I even been to a school football game, dance, or other major social event. In many ways, Chuck and Karen did not see these activities as essential to the general goal of academic excellence. There are no set guidelines to raising children. Therefore, it really is on a case-by-case basis. In my particular situation, I think they made the right decisions. History has certainly proven them correct! Considering the personality traits that they had to contend with in my character over the years, their strictness paid off. I am truly grateful for it.

It is no wonder that they expressed extreme skepticism when I approached them with the idea of entering the Student Government

Association (SGA) campaign for president. They voiced their concern that, while the effort might indeed be exciting, how prepared was I for defeat? As any good parents, they did not want me to suffer; yet, they also did not want to inhibit my dreams. They expressed realism and shared their opinions so that I could make an informed decision. In the end, they granted their consent and support but cautioned me in my optimism. It must be understood that I led two lives — one at school and one at home. There were numerous times that other parents had championed me as an ideal role model, unbeknownst to my own family. Yet Chuck and Karen were not out of touch with my school life; it was just that their busy careers in medicine clouded their perspective. That would all change.

Not only did I win the race against the three most eligible opponents; the smartest guy, the most popular guy, and the most experienced student government guy in school; I did so without a runoff – the first in Jesuit's history! With the help of friends and an organized campaign effort, I became SGA president for my senior year. In the end, my campaign speech espousing honesty and dedication to school spirit won the day. My sincerity showed through and apparently touched the hearts and minds of all the student body, not just my particular class.

Chuck and Karen were pleased. However, it caused a major shift in my social activities. My presence was now expected at all school functions; well, *that was at least the impression I created at home.* My new position was pivotal to the organization and coordination of student activities. As long as I maintained my grades, there was little criticism that could be voiced at home. In short, the year was a smashing success academically and socially. I achieved a 4.0 average for the year, orchestrated six school dances resulting in the largest SGA treasury in years, and became respected and admired by my peers. The position catapulted me socially and helped heal prejudices from my past. In addition, serving on our school's award-winning Quiz Bowl team helped seal my newfound popularity. Upon graduation, my life certainly seemed on a stellar rise.

*   *   *   *

Unlike many of my peers, I did not partake in the lure of alcohol consumption in high school. Predominately due to the loving and structured home life I was blessed to have in the Campbell household. Chuck and Karen were very clear that they did not approve nor would they tolerate any degree of underage drinking under their roof. Being in the medical profession they witnessed the incessant slew of tragedies caused by DWIs, alcoholic parents, and accidental deaths or life altering injuries that resulted from the influence of alcohol. In fact alcohol was never a regular staple at family gatherings. Granted, on very special occasions adults consumed but never to excess. On numerous evenings I was privy to stories of anonymous patients my parents encountered whose lives were irreversibly changed because they succumbed to inebriated excesses. These tragic tales left a lasting impression; furthermore, the numerous friends or associates that made up our family's circle of friends never demonstrated a penchant for alcohol. These individuals were not teetotalers, on the contrary, but rather partook within "social norms."

I will not deny that my initial encounters with drinking did occur towards the end of my senior year in high school. There were occasions of a celebratory nature such as prom and graduation where the opportunity presented itself, the risk seemed minimal, and I maintained a conscientious control that permitted a reserved indulgence. Unlike many of my classmates, my participation in or attendance at "senior parties" was unacceptable. I am deeply grateful to Chuck and Karen for their firm parental guidance in this area and for their zero tolerance of underage consumption! NO, seriously I mean that!

Frequently, while listening to the endless stories of my fellow students and their weekend activities, I felt out of touch and in some ways deprived of the colorful social lives of my friends. Wild boisterous tales of joyrides, drinking games, promiscuous encounters with the opposite sex, and jovial camaraderie were all the rage on Monday mornings at school following partying weekends. Feelings of regret and paranoia at being perceived as a prude or a nerd regularly plagued my thoughts. In my mind the only consolation was that I fortunately avoided the routine amount of trouble that always seemed to follow closely behind such "fun times." My senior year brought some relief to my anguish, for as SGA president my token attendance or involvement in almost every aspect of Loyola school functions was required — *or at least I made sure of that.* I must confess the desire to run for student body president was not limited to my unselfish interest of being a school leader or role model, but the ulterior motive of broadening my social interactions and extracurricular activities lurking just below the surface.

Two particular stories are still prevalent with me today. As they were related to me via third party I have no guarantee that the details are truly accurate. Nonetheless as the hearsay would have it the first story was ironically humorous while the second was erotically intriguing. In many ways they both demonstrate to what degree I and my fellow classmates lived rather carefree lives within an insulated bubble of privilege.

One of my classmates, we'll call him Aaron, was one of the guys I truly admired and looked up to as the kind of fellow I wished I could be. Aaron was from a wealthy family, cool, athletic, good looking, and quite popular. Towards the end of our senior year word traveled quickly that Aaron had planned to host one "of the maddest" senior parties in Shreveport history. The event was to take place on a weekend while Aaron's parents were out of town. To say the least, Aaron's parents were completely unaware of the planned festivities. From all accounts everyone who was anyone was there. There was a "hot" rock band, countless kegs of beer, and an endless supply of good food. The best part of this historical senior party was that Aaron's home was located in a rather secluded rural suburb of town, easily providing cover from the police. For that matter, there was little chance any neighbors would be disturbed or inadvertently report back to Aaron's parents. Everything seemed to go according to plan: the party was a huge success; no one was injured or arrested. By the time Aaron's parents returned on Sunday there was no evidence whatsoever that a party had even taken place — or so Aaron thought! He was completely confident, almost smug even, that they were no more the wiser. However, shortly after their return, Aaron's father called for him to come downstairs into the living room. Aaron entered the room "happy as a lark" until he noticed the stern look upon his father's face and his mother's gaze upwards towards the ceiling. As Aaron followed her line of sight up to the crystal chandelier he could not help but notice the huge chunk of cheesy pepperoni pizza dangling from one of the sparkling bulbs. Rumor had it that Aaron was grounded and severely scolded for the betrayal of his parents' trust.

My second story involves one of the more notorious pranksters in our graduating class; let's call him Sean. Now Sean's family was not just wealthy, they were what most people would refer to as "filthy rich!" Supposedly upon their relocation to Shreveport Sean's mother located the home of her choice in one of Shreveport's more affluent neighborhoods, paid half a million dollars cash on site, and spent another half million furnishing it to her taste. Shortly after Sean's transfer to Loyola his father, as a gesture of appreciation and loyal support, donated an entire weight room full of top of the line universal exercise equipment for the football team's use; Sean had just become a member. Throughout his two years as a member of the student body Sean's exploits were legendary both on and off the field. One such story recounted the real facts surrounding his recent stay in the hospital for injuries supposedly sustained from an automobile accident. Truth be told, according to the grapevine, Sean and his female passenger had been slightly injured while engaged in an act of oral sex that resulted in a head on collision of his Mercedes with a tree. To show their displeasure his parents punished Sean for his carelessness and reckless behavior: they took away his Mercedes and forced him to drive a rundown Audi for the rest of his school term!

I recount these two particular incidents to loosely demonstrate that I and my classmates lived in another era and by most accounts had very privileged and sheltered lives. As SGA president, I too was "expected" to do my part in the year-long celebrations of our senior year and for our impending graduation. Any such inebriated or debauchery free for all was not only out of the question but would have occurred only "when hell froze over!" To Chuck and Karen's credit I must admit they were understanding and gracious in making allowances to accommodate my social obligations as "leader of the student body." They agreed to permit me to host a "senior party" according to their specific guidelines: one, the invitation list was limited to 35 of my classmates and or their dates; two, there would be no loud music and definitely no drinking; three, the evening would be a semi-dinner party rather than a rock 'n roll fest. My initial response was hesitant horror! As far as I knew nothing like that had ever been attempted or, for that matter, even conceived as a "real senior party." Furthermore, I was horrified at the prospect of choosing who to invite and who to exclude.

Reluctantly, I narrowed my list of invitees down to 35 classmates, personally delivered the invitations, and nervously awaited the response. To my ultimate surprise and desperate sigh of relief the response was overwhelming. All 35 invitees responded rather positively and even expressed a degree of anticipation to the event. I had no idea what an overwhelming success the evening would be. Every iota of credit must be given to Karen for her creative plans and tireless preparations. Playing the role of nervous and somewhat apprehensive host, I had some serious doubts as to the eventual success of my "senior party." Furthermore, my paranoia as to how my classmates would respond to a "dinner party for young adults" was rampant. I should have had more faith in Karen and my friends!

I certainly expected the guys and their dates to attend. However, I primarily anticipated their token appearances to be friendly, cordial, and most of all short lived. For the most part many of them had never been to my home or met my parents. As I've said before, my social life was virtually nonexistent: at least it was nothing like I had heard or imagined my fellow students to be like. During the entire evening and afternoon before the party, I was a nervous wreck — like a chicken with its head cut off! Thanks to Karen's detailed planning and experience as the consummate hostess I had nothing to worry about. All morning and afternoon of that day she patiently guided, suggested, and directed all of the necessary preparations. The house was immaculate and the menu was perfectly prepped. I had never been so proud!

Anticipating the culinary preferences of teenagers, Karen had brilliantly planned a "make your own" pizza party! She had premade 80 personal pan pizza crusts, homemade of course; expertly directed me in the preparation of every possible pizza topping a teenager could possibly desire; and carefully organized the kitchen layout so as to provide the ideal setting for each guest to either make their own or oversee the crafting of their personal pizza by another. Throughout the evening our kitchen and dining room was a regular assembly line allowing for one shift after another of cooks and consumers. Beyond belief, the entire process moved smoothly with almost mechanized precision! If I had not seen it for myself I would never have believed it. In between shifts, our guests mingled from room to room as if they were adults just like their parents. Throughout the evening my friends remarked repeatedly what a unique idea and how absolutely wonderful a time they were having.

As I had indicated, unlike the drunken beer fests of other such events, this "senior party" was intentionally alcohol free. A wide assortment of sodas and fruit juices was available throughout the evening to quench our insatiable thirst. However, halfway through the evening I caught a glimpse of Chuck whizzing through the crowd and out the front door. The cold stern expression upon his face left little doubt that trouble was not far behind. I gradually meandered my way to the living room where Karen very discreetly pulled me aside to explain. Apparently one of my guests had repeatedly disappeared to return to his car for some "substitute libation." She advised me to carry on normally so as not to neglect my other guests while reassuring me that Chuck would take care of everything. I could not help but worry, naturally assuming the worst. Shortly thereafter he returned to the party, smiling, nonchalantly explaining that everything was fine. He did note however, that one of our guests unfortunately had to leave early and would not be returning. Later that evening, Chuck described in detail how he had followed the young man out to his car and discovered him adding alcohol to a soft drink. It was at this point that he requested my classmate to discard the drink, cautioned him to drive home carefully, and politely thanked him for coming. With that, there was no further discussion of the incident other than for Chuck to apologize for his regrettable yet necessary actions.

My success as SGA president had certainly caught the eye of the faculty and administration as well. In recognition of my efforts, I was awarded the prestigious Daughters of the American Revolution Good Citizen Award by our local Member of Congress, Charles "Buddy" Roemer. That introduction would cement our personal friendship and open new doors to enhance my growing interest in politics. In addition, high school graduation night would be only a repetition of my successful grammar school equivalent. Again, I had to use my hardbound diploma as a tray for the numerous awards I received. Honors in history, almost a full scholarship to the college I had chosen — Centenary College of Louisiana, as well as the highest award at Jesuit — the Flyer of the Year, once again proved that my mom and Joy Campbell had made the right decision in asking Chuck and Karen to raise me. All of my successes over the last six years were living proof that God, through each of these angels, had granted me *A Second Chance*.

*   *   *   *

My first recollection of any serious experience with alcohol was graduation night. One of my classmates had a celebratory get together at his home to mark the end of our high school years. If my memory serves me correctly, I imbibed a couple of glasses of well-deserved champagne. For one so inexperienced with alcohol, those few glasses of "bubbly" left me "buzzed" to say the least. The experience was neither remarkable or memorable except that "being under the influence" dramatically tore down the defensive walls I had so carefully constructed to protect myself and my reputation from ridicule. Numerous classmates seemed to enjoy the transformation of my character from stoic and reserved to lively and "cool." Such camaraderie with my peers was a welcome change of pace. To be accepted and regarded "as one of the guys" was for me a dream come true. In my opinion for so many youth, peer acceptance during these transformational years is the quintessential goal of high school socialization. It is no wonder then that peer pressure has such a dramatic influence over our character and personality during the formative teenage years. This influence can supersede good judgment, parental guidance, and basic common sense to the point of self-destructive behavior.

Unfortunately during these formative years the emotional and psychological foundations of the human psyche are still untested and underdeveloped to provide the individual with a reliable base of decision making principles. To further complicate the narrative, there is no "set in stone" age classification to clearly delineate the moment when an individual reaches the age of wisdom. Society, through a haphazard trial and error methodology, has attempted to legally define the moment when a person reaches adulthood, i.e., the legal drinking age of 21. It is ironic however, that in the United States an individual can legally vote for the highest office in the land or willingly lay down his or her life in defense of the nation at age 18, but is prohibited by law from having the emotional wherewithal to responsibly consume alcohol. Such distortions in the fabric of society only further serve to confuse the developing minds of our youth – but I digress. My tentative experimentation with drinking rapidly progressed from ad hoc to habitual. During the brief summer hiatus between high school and college, the thrill and hypnotic draw of alcohol consumption was greatly influenced by a broadening of my horizons; from the regimented life of academic pursuit to the more carefree and somewhat less constrained world of gainful employment. Chuck had made it quite clear that, unlike previous summer breaks; I would seek, obtain, and hold on to a full time job. Shortly after graduation, primarily due to the influential recommendation of a family friend, I began working as a glorified "car hop" at Portland's Dry Cleaners. Highly regarded as the finest dry cleaner in the Shreveport/ Bossier area, this fine establishment maintained a regular crew of between 15 and 20 college age males whose primary function was to ensure that no customer was inconvenienced by having to get out of their cars. As one can imagine, such dedicated customer service guaranteed elite, as well as an adoring teenage female, clientele. To say that such a testosterone charged environment was influential is an understatement – in more ways than one. Though Chuck and Karen's careful and deliberate guidance protected me from the catastrophic perils substance abuse can often deliver, no parental protection can be infinite especially after "leaving the nest," as I would soon discover.

8

CLOAKED AND DRUNKARD

CENTENARY COLLEGE RESIDES in the heart of Shreveport on a beautifully landscaped campus covering approximately 2 square miles. It had a reputation for being one of the finest liberal arts colleges of its size in the nation. Noted as the oldest liberal arts college west of the Mississippi founded in 1825, the Centennial of United Methodist church founder John Wesley's death. Though Tufts University in Boston was my first choice for a college education, with Georgetown in Washington, DC coming in a close second, my selection of Centenary was one I shall never regret. In many ways it was "a no brainer" of the contenders. Located in my hometown, directly across the street from the Campbell's (my "guardian" grandparents) it was an ideal choice.

Furthermore, through a fortunate turn of luck I was blessed to have received a nearly "full ride" of academic scholarships from the quiz bowl. During my senior year at Loyola I had participated on the quiz bowl championship team competing in the Fabsteel sponsored tournament which Centenary hosted on a local television station. Though we came in second place for a five state region the prize was still a sizeable complement of academic scholarships for the team membership. The said fortunate turn of luck was that I wound up being the only teammate seriously considering attending Centenary. Therefore, I received the total allotment of scholarship prize money. The final feather in my cap was the personal recommendation from one of the doctors Karen worked with at Schumpert Hospital. Dr. "G's" recommendation carried a great deal of weight because his family had been extremely generous contributors to the college's endowment. For the last several decades one or more members of his family had served on Centenary's Board of Trustees and Dr. "G" himself was a revered alumnus. For many years he and I had become well acquainted with each other because of our mutual participation as volunteers/patrons of the Shreveport Summer Music Festival. Not only did he write a glowing recommendation for my entrance application, but as an added plus, he strongly urged Chuck and Karen to grant me the opportunity of fully experiencing college life by living on campus in a dormitory. I will always be deeply grateful to Dr. "G!" for his significant friendship in this regard.

Like so many institutions of higher learning, Open House weekend was purposefully designed to be the clinching element in convincing a prospective student that Centenary was the right choice. Naturally there were the standard campus tours promoting the various academic departments, intentionally prepared choice menus at every meal function, a Saturday night social mixer/dance, and of course the late hour introductory Greek parties at each respective social fraternity/sorority house. The whole weekend was an absolute blast of a good time and the entire experience easily convinced me that Centenary was the college for me.

The whole moving into the dorm scene was a combination of excitement and trepidation. I think it was a mutual bag of emotions for Chuck and Karen as well. For weeks they had helped me gather together many of the accessories I would require for life on my own in the dorm. Karen had carefully collected towels, pots and pans, dishes, and other such items to ease me into this state of transition. My parents had even graciously paid the $25 application fee as a sign of support for my decision to attend Centenary. Monetarily speaking, that would be the only expenditure of actual cash they would make towards my college education. The move in to Cline Hall was amid a flurry of repeated trips up and down flights of stairs by us and other families sending their kids off to school. With the final box unloaded there was a quiet unsettling pause between the three of us as we realized that the moment had come to bid farewell. A strong firm handshake with Chuck and a pat on my back, an affectionate clutching embrace and kiss with Karen, some slight tears of mixed emotion, a hearty "have fun and we'll see you soon" and they were gone. The silence was deafening. I felt simultaneously exhilarated that I was on my own and yet extremely uneasy about the future that lay ahead.

Shortly after my parents departed, I met my first college dorm mate, David. He was nice, soft spoken, slightly effeminate, and his persona seemed to indicate some deeply hidden pain. I would never fully discover the reason for David's obviously troubled past. In short, over the course of the one semester we roomed together our paths crossed infrequently and certainly to no degree that we became good friends. I can tell you he was at Centenary on a choir scholarship, was pursuing general studies, previously lived with his grandparents and very younger "stepbrother," wasn't much of a partier, and at times seemed like "a fish out of water." Between Thanksgiving and Christmas breaks David withdrew from school because of "troubles at home." One of his last nights on campus, under the slight influence of alcohol, he secretly admitted to me that the "stepbrother" was in reality his own illegitimate son that he had fathered as a result of a one night stand with an older woman when he was just 15. He confessed, in almost teary sadness, that the traumatic experience had scarred him for life. He loved his son dearly but doubted he could ever be a suitable father. David's unexpected withdrawal from school was relayed to me by the office of the Dean of students. I've not seen or spoken with him since. His story demonstrates that *personal adversity from your past can indeed dramatically affect your future.*

Though David's sudden departure provided me with quiet solitude for the end of term exams, it did create a sudden financial problem: I could not afford a private room. As it would turn out an acquaintance of mine, Rob was also in need of a roommate for the coming spring semester. This was a remarkable coincidence considering the two of us lived in the same "suite." Cline Hall was certainly the most preferred male dormitory on campus. Consisting of approximately 380 rooms, its architectural design was the most unique. Cline was three stories high surrounding a cobblestone open air courtyard. Each doorway leading off the courtyard opened onto a short hallway with two rooms on both sides and a communal bathroom at the end. This was a "suite" and our number was 2A.

To say that Rob and David were complete opposites would be a gross understatement. Rob at times could be loud, boisterous, and "in your face." His claim to fame was that he was an excellent soccer player for the college team. Hailing from Baton Rouge, Louisiana, he was an avid fan of the hard rock group AC/DC. From the very beginning I knew our friendship as dorm mates would be a far cry from that of my previous one. I liked Rob because in many ways his fast paced hard driving attitude about life was just what I needed to come out of my shell; though at the time I didn't know it. Being Rob's dorm mate brought me into close association with the entire membership of the Centenary soccer team. During my tenure at Centenary they were without a doubt the coolest and most popular group on campus. It was an honor for me to be accepted among their circle of friends. It was this camaraderie that reunited me with a former acquaintance; Mark K. Mark had been a friend of a friend whom I had known during the latter years of high school. Thanks to my friendship with Rob and Mark, the spring semester of my freshman year in college brought remarkable changes in my life. During that single semester I began an intense effort to work out, joined the staff of the college newspaper, *The Conglomerate*, became an avid fan of the rock band U2, went to my first rock concert, began a regular practice of drinking, joined a musician's fraternity, and broadly expanded my social life.

Privately, I was determined to overcome personal doubts as to the true nature of my self-identity. In other words all of my endeavors were a subconscious attempt to become "one of the guys." I was so convinced that my previous experiences with "my mentor" and disparaging rumors spread by jerks that were just jealous of my success, were all part of a state of confusion in my adolescent search for self-awareness. Like so many other guys I drank, partied, and chased girls. The drive, to be like so many of my friends, was a natural reaction; to overcome self-conscious guilt regarding the private thoughts I rationalized were caused by the actions of "my mentor" so many years before.

This may well explain why in such a brief amount of time I transformed from someone who really had no interest in drinking to an out of control probable alcoholic. Throughout that semester there were innumerable occasions I completely passed out from alcohol consumption.

As a Japanese proverb goes, *"first the man takes a drink, then the drink takes a drink, then the drink takes the man."* Addiction takes many forms and affects many people differently. There is alcohol addiction, there is drug addiction, there is sex addiction, there's addiction to power, there is greed, and the list goes on. Each addiction has varying degrees and a multitude of results. In addition, an individual's genetic makeup and environmental influences contribute greatly to how far one falls from grace. In my case many factors have contributed to struggles with alcohol and drugs. In many ways I am more fortunate than most because of the endless number of loved ones, friends, and simple acquaintances who have given me a network of support.

During all my years at Centenary I was fortuitously employed on a consistent basis at Portland's Cleaners. I was exposed to numerous influences affecting my character socially, professionally, and psychologically. Providing quality customer service to many of the community's economic, political, and social elite honed many of the public relations and work ethic skills I still cherish to this day. Over the years I was able to garner a high degree of sincere respect and adoration from many of our customers. The gradual development of rapport served me well for many years to come. I cannot adequately count the number of influential relationships that my employment at Portland's successfully achieved on my behalf. My customers included well respected academics, influential politicians, and countless captains of industry. Furthermore, I came to greatly appreciate the undeniable influence of these individuals' spouses. It is perhaps here that I first coined the phrase "*Who* you know gets you in the door. *What* you know keeps you there!" Over the years many of these customer service relationships would dramatically transpire into successful community service partnerships in academics, politics, and the arts.

Only now in hindsight can I honestly recognize an equally influential aspect of my time working at Portland's: namely, the increasingly overpowering effect of drinking and partying with my coworkers after work hours. Simultaneously, the lack of parental control of college life while living in the dorm only further maximized the gradually deteriorating effect on me as a whole. Reluctantly, Chuck and Karen had agreed with Dr. "G's" suggestion that my college experience would be better served by living on campus rather than at home, despite the fact that we lived only mere miles from the college.

All the years of protective parental guidance had sheltered me from the destructive influence of alcohol. Suddenly within a period of a few months I was bombarded by the dramatically powerful influence of peer pressure and unrestricted access to alcohol. The lure of unregulated socialized drinking took its toll on me personally, socially, and academically. Were it not for the foundations of good character so carefully laid by the Campbell family years before, the results of this excessive alcoholic free for all may very well have been terminal.

As with most college freshman, the first semester's Rush week had been a nonstop cascade of rock 'n roll dancing, keg parties, and stumbling from one frat house to the next with beer in hand in the pursuit of peer acceptance. At Centenary there were five national fraternities represented and two national sororities. I must admit that there were very strong influences drawing me towards Kappa Sigma. Many of the underclassmen that I had become friends with seemed to be veering in that direction. Furthermore, their house and active members appealed to me as the Greek group that I felt most comfortable with. However, there were two distinct factors inhibiting my immediate acceptance among Kappa Sigma's membership. Firstly, from a historical perspective the college's fraternities had been a constant thorn in Joy Campbell's side for years due to the close proximity of my godmother/grandmother's home to fraternity row. Over the years, she had acquired quite a reputation among the Greeks as a nuisance. To say the least, they're noisy and boisterous parties wreaked havoc on her quiet home life less than 1000 yards from her front door. She could be counted on as the first neighbor to complain to the administration about the incessant late night loud music and drunken partying. I found it somewhat humorous, that once the fact was known of my relationship to Joy Campbell, my notoriety seemed to increase. There can be no doubt this was primarily due to an expectation that I would have a significantly positive influence to curb her criticisms of their leisurely activities. They obviously expected too much and were sadly disappointed to discover I would have little influence over Mrs. Campbell's opinion.

Secondly, several active members of this particular chapter of Kappa Sigma fraternity were alumni of both my grade school and high school. Shortly after my declaration to become a member of the pledge class, slight rumblings began to reverberate through the active members expressing concerns and doubts as to my worthiness of membership in their revered brotherhood. Suggestions were made that my consideration should be delayed until the spring semester for a more careful and thorough evaluation by the active members. I came to learn through the grapevine that certain actives had blatantly questioned the essence of my sexuality. They pointed to rumors and innuendos from the past that they had either heard or initiated themselves. Naturally, the Kappa Sigs were hesitant and felt more time was required to know me better. Some of my pledge class were angry and entertained the idea of dropping out of the fraternity's rush schedule to show their support on my behalf. One in particular, Dean, was emphatic in this regard: to him I am eternally grateful for his loyalty and friendship. Dean's demonstration was the only consoling fact throughout this whole ordeal. However, I graciously withdrew my pledging to Kappa Sigma promising to renew in the spring; my intentions were sincere despite this severe blow to my reputation and ego.

This setback in my college career plans resulted in an overzealous crusade to prove myself to the fraternity and others. There wasn't a frat party or social event on campus that I didn't attend or close down without winding up in a drunken stupor.

As I mentioned earlier my second semester in college brought changes in my dorm mate situation. Rob and I had gotten to know each other during our first semester through our mutual classes and one drunken stupor after another. He and I seemed to make a natural team. My point is that such a friendship naturally led to an increased amount of drinking and partying unlike any I had ever known in my entire life. For example, Rob was the friend that taught me how to play "quarters." When we started both of us drank shots of beer. By midterm in the semester Rob was still drinking shots of beer but I had graduated to straight shots of vodka. In addition I became good friends with other members of the soccer team and did my best to live up to their standard of socializing. It must be made perfectly clear that this increased alcohol consumption was my own doing and that despite my associations with others who drank profusely, the ultimate decision to partake was my choice. Furthermore, Centenary College had a policy of prohibiting the possession of or consumption of alcohol on "campus grounds". Granted, this policy did not extend to any of the Greek houses and there were never any inspections of our dorm rooms. Unfortunately, my drinking was totally out of control. By the end of the spring semester alcohol consumption wasn't a routine but rather a way of life.

Over spring break my parents issued an ultimatum that I would move back home or they would cut me off and I would be completely on my own. Upon returning to the campus I made the first "adult" decision of my young life and refused to accept Chuck and Karen's terms. Within the hour of my refusal Grandpa Campbell appeared at my dormitory and demanded, at the request of my mom and dad, both sets of house keys to the family homes. With tears in his eyes, he remarked how sorry he was that the situation had come to this end, but that it was necessary and the whole family was united in their opinion that I was out of control. For days I was in absolute shock and disbelief. Yet my dismay still did not diminish my ravenous thirst for liquor. If anything, it only dulled the "pleasurable" experience of drinking until I was blind drunk.

That spring semester of 1984 also marked another first for me... my first sexual relationship with the opposite sex. Ironically, it was initiated the night of my first political campaign loss by a completely unexpected source. The night I suffered an embarrassing defeat in the student government senate race to a seemingly "air headed" sorority girl, my intentions were to console myself into a drunken stupor. Following the disappointing news of my defeat, I, a new fraternity brother, and two female companions decided to kick back with a couple of bottles of champagne. Although initially intended to be a victory celebration, the evening quickly spiraled into a pity party. Shortly after finishing the first bottle, we all decided to take a joy ride to a nearby city park. Once there my date, Pam, suggested that she and I should take a walk.

We ended up on the very top of the rocket slide gradually finishing off our half of the champagne. Buzzing, and completely clueless as to her real intentions, I remember vaguely just standing there gazing into the night sky. She very calmly asked "do you know what you need?" And I responded in a rather aggravated tone, "No! What do I need?" The next thing I know, she rather deftly unbuttoned my jeans and proceeded to orally pleasure me. Considering the evening's turn of events, my current state of inebriation, and the complete unexpected nature of her actions I am surprised everything turned out as well as it did. Over the next several months she and I dated and continued our rather heated physical affair to greater and greater heights. Being a few years older than I and certainly more experienced, Pam taught me a great deal.

My first sexual relationship with a woman ended quite abruptly. Initially I believed it was due to a mistaken accusation by me that Pam had given me a sexually transmitted disease (STD). The truth of the matter, after seeking professional medical expertise, was that I had simply contracted a yeast infection from her. For an inexperienced sexual novice such as me, the resulting symptoms of a yeast infection and an STD can be remarkably similar. She was understandably insulted at my accusation and even more condescending upon learning of the actual cause to my physical predicament. Only weeks later would I learn the actual reason for the abrupt end to our hot and heavy romance. I was completely stunned to discover, while downing a couple of six packs with my good buddy Mark K, that he also had lost his virginity to an older student named Pam. After a few minutes of initial shock the two of us could not help but laugh ourselves silly at the notion that we unknowingly had been seduced by the same older "chick." To say the least, that mutually shared experience is one of many reasons why I consider Mark to be my very best friend — the big brother I never had. This "adversity" of being jilted by my very *first* female sex partner *and* the dreadful fear of contracting an STD after that *first* "straight" sexual relationship should have taught me that "love" can be fleeting and that one can never be "too careful" with regards to sex. Unfortunately I did not learn my lesson, as the future will prove. I did learn however, that throughout our lives real friendships last longer than meaningless physical relationships!

During that summer I simply replaced my regular drinking buddies, my classmates, with my coworkers from Portland's Cleaners. I distinctly remember on two separate occasions blacking out; one night in particular showing up at my coworker's home wrapped in a soiled ragged blanket stumbling up the driveway with no recollection of where I had been or how I had gotten there.

For the first time in my life I had no home to go to; I lived on campus throughout the summer requiring me to box, store, and totally relocate all of my possessions from dorm room to dorm room as one session began and another ended. I was totally on my own, even though I had made amends with my parents before they moved north to Pennsylvania. There was no way my meager income through part time employment at Portland's would come even close to covering all of my expenses for tuition, housing, meals, and books. Though I had scholarships, some of these were for a limited time and were restricted to cover only academic expenses. Therefore, I was forced to seek assistance by other means such as Pell grants and low interest government student loans. Nonetheless, through the experienced expertise of Centenary's financial aid office I was able to continue my collegiate education while living on campus all year long throughout my five year tenure at the college. With some degree of pride I can claim that I put myself through college without the financial assistance of my parents, though ending up a great deal in debt. None of it would have been possible without the assistance, support, and the sincere belief so many people, my family included, had in my personal character.

My defeat for the student Senate coupled with my close association with Rob, Mark, and the soccer team helped to bolster my endeavors as a regular contributing member of the college newspaper staff. By the beginning of my sophomore year personnel changes at *The Conglomerate* resulted in my rapid ascension to the position of Editor in chief. My responsibilities included layout design, advertising acquisition, copy editing, staff management, bookkeeping, routine progress reports to the student government, and delegation of story assignments for the monthly production of Centenary's multi page newspaper. This position brought me into daily contact and sometimes confrontational encounters, with students, faculty, staff, and the administration.

In addition to my responsibilities as head of the newspaper I had also become the co-chairman/co-founder of the campus' chapter of College Republicans. In many ways this should have been viewed by me as a highly unethical conflict of interest – partisan political control of the press. However, at the time my numerous political contacts assured me that the combination was an extremely advantageous partnership to garner support for the upcoming Reagan/Bush re-election campaign. My simultaneous stewardship of these two campus organizations resulted in three distinct memorable occurrences. The first was the unprecedented inclusion as a member of the selected press corps to cover Vice President George H.W. Bush's campaign visit to the Shreveport/Bossier area. Accompanied by my good friend/fraternity brother/staff photographer Scott, we joined seasoned correspondents from all the major media outlets on the press bus as part of the presidential motorcade. It was indeed an honor to have the opportunity of asking a direct question to the second highest officeholder in the land. Scott's photo layout and my corresponding news coverage took up two entire pages of a *Conglomerate* special edition.

The other two memorable episodes were not so positive, but extremely educational. As chairman of the College Republican chapter I was responsible for setting an agenda of key issues upon which to focus our chapter's campaign efforts. In addition to promoting the Republican Party's stands on strong national defense and fiscal economic reform, it was also decided that we should pay closer attention to controversial social issues like homosexuality. In hindsight I must admit that my staunch support for attacking this particular issue was highly hypocritical, and privately to a greater degree more of an effort to divert attention from my own personal conflict. I now am highly embarrassed that I ever participated in such a prejudicial effort to disparage any of my fellow classmates! However, I am proud to admit that I was wrong — *another example of how adversity in later life can cause us, through self reflection, to admit our past mistakes and be deeply humbled by them.*

This staunchly right wing corruption of the campus media resulted in a very terse and rebuking letter to the editor ironically authored by the name of Andrew Jackson. Immediately jumping to conclusion without proper research or verification, the hallmark of good journalism, I quickly penned a nasty reply. My response defiantly accused the writer of cowardice for lacking the courage to sign his/her real name to the negative attack. It never occurred to me that the student's real name was in actuality Andrew Jackson! To say that I was both surprised and highly embarrassed when the student confronted me face to face with his state issued driver's license bearing the actual name of Andrew Jackson, is an understatement. In all fairness I printed a retraction and an apology, but it was a well-deserved lesson in humility! Now and then a "swift kick in the seat of our pants" can go a long way in helping us build character.

Another lesson in humiliating hindsight regarding my public abhorrence to homosexuality involves my experiences with fraternal organizations—namely, Kappa Sigma and Phi Mu Alpha Sinfonia. Having first been denied acceptance as a pledge for Kappa Sigma during the Rush season of my freshman year because of rumor and innuendo, I agreed to accept the invitation by the music fraternity Phi Mu Alpha Sinfonia. The chapter president, Ben, had heard of my involvement with the Shreveport Summer Music Festival and suggested that my obvious love of music might be a good fit with their organization's primary purposes. They were in no way deterred by my lack of music proficiency but were rather enthusiastically supportive of my efforts to promote musical performance. I was highly honored and eagerly accepted their offer to join. Becoming a Sinfonian is without a doubt one of the greatest honors of my life! However, I am ashamed to admit that my acceptance into this hallowed brotherhood was conditional upon the ejection of one of their own because of his sexual advances towards me at a fraternity function. In the fraternity we have a phrase that stresses once a brother, always a brother. To the chapter membership I made it quite clear it was either him or me. Though his advances were inappropriate, my response and ultimatum were equally unacceptable. I will forever regret that I shunned a fellow brother and hypocritically demanded his expulsion. Should I ever have the opportunity, I would humbly ask for his forgiveness.

I have made mention of these transcendental moments in my early college years to stress the degree to which I was driven to convince myself and others of whom Tom Ufert really was. Despite underlying signals to the contrary, there was no question in my mind that I was the typical heterosexual male. Any and all doubts of my sexual orientation were convincingly rationalized away as simple subconscious curiosities that afflict every young man "trying to find himself." These excuses were further reinforced by my keen interest and desire to become sexually involved with the opposite sex, which materialized into actual experiences with at least a dozen girls and women. Furthermore, my sometimes vitriolic crusade to publicly rebuke all things homosexual was only further evidence, in my mind, that I had to be "straight." In the gay community this is referred to as "deeply closeted." A "deeply closeted" guy will frequently strike out so harshly and sometimes violently, at the very thing he himself is personally ashamed of. This behavior can lead down a self-destructive path of alcohol or drug abuse, crime, physical or psychological abuse, and even suicide. Sometimes there are life altering experiences that temporarily divert one's attention and motivation so completely that the true moment of awakening to reality is only further postponed. One such event was Mother's Day, 1985.

9
GOODBYE MOM

THERE ARE CERTAIN events in all of our lives that we will do almost anything to forget. We will build an endless barrier of walls within our subconscious to block out the pain and keep others at a distance. This chapter in my life is one such event.

I really didn't want to go. It had been a couple of months since I had *found enough time* to see her. I was 19 and it was the spring of my second year in college. Oh the impatience of youth and our façade of invincibility! Living only seven blocks from Centenary College (on "Merrick" street no less; reminding me constantly of John Merrick, "the Elephant Man"), my mom was living the best life she could with MS. Some could call it barely existing. She was completely wheelchair bound and totally dependent upon the assistance of others. Every waking minute required another person to perform the everyday functions we take for granted. She could not independently transfer in or out of her heavy metal wheelchair. Therefore someone had to help her with getting in and out of bed, dressing, feeding, bathing, toiletries, etc…Mom's life was what most of us would consider hell. Thank God there was Dudley,

Earthaleen, Joy and Charles. Especially Dudley! His death would prove to be a noble selfless act of undying friendship.

Where was the rest of Gloria Ufert's family, myself included? We were hiding! We were all, in our own ways, hiding from the reality of who and what Mom had become in the wake of multiple sclerosis. The tragedy was too much for most of us to handle on a daily basis; yet, Mom struggled through with the last shred of independence she had. Succumbing to the antiseptic world of assisted living in a nursing home rather than living "independently" in a house; she would have crawled up and died. Dudley Somner made her only independence possible. Nanny and Grandpa still lived in Cedar Grove, clear on the other side of town, visiting infrequently. Caru was now residing with husband number two, William, and a young daughter Maddie in the DC area. Me? I lived in a dormitory some seven blocks away. This was certainly a case of "out of sight, out of mind." Having said that, it is truly shameful that friends rather than family were the only hope Mom had. The Campbells lived only six blocks away and either Joy or Charles made a concerted effort to visit every day and see to it that my mom was okay. Thank God for true friends!

It was Mother's Day, 1985. My spring semester was winding down with exams and papers. The upcoming summer was full of exciting adventure and promised to be most advantageous for my extracurricular life. It was already confirmed that within a year I would be working on Capitol Hill in D.C. as a Lyndon B. Johnston Congressional intern, and my plans for riding Amtrak across the eastern US offered me the opportunity to broaden my horizons. In addition, a weeklong fraternity national assembly in Atlanta, Georgia, also promised up and coming stature for me socially. This combined to give me an all-encompassing and totally self-absorbed air of ambivalence toward seeing my mom on Mother's Day. Looking back I am totally ashamed of my lack of love and compassion. Mrs. Campbell always came to my aid by emphasizing that a young man has to move on with his life and pursue those things that will help him get ahead. She always seemed to make excuses for me, understanding how awful it was to see a person you love, dying day by day. In hindsight, though, I am grateful for her understanding and sheltering nature. Yet my shame remains, for I did love Mom and failed to show her how much. My actions unfortunately spoke boomingly louder than my words. There will always be a son's pondering of "what if's" that might or might not have affected the outcome of that fateful week.

The Campbell's almost froze in horror at my failure to want to visit Mom. Rightfully so, they felt that it would be unforgivable for me to let this particular holiday pass without so much as even an hour with Mom. I am so grateful that they "twisted my arm" and insisted I see her. There are key moments in a man's life when he must do what's right regardless of personal feelings *because* it is the right thing to do. Furthermore, there are personal sacrifices that truly are trivial in comparison to the joy and happiness we bring our loved ones. It is hard sometimes to do the right thing, but it is *never* hard to know what the right thing *is*; that little voice in the back of your head never fails. Mother's Day, 1985, will forever be enshrined in my life as such a moment — a moment when you are glad that someone helped you follow that little voice.

Words cannot describe the nervous hesitation I felt before turning the doorknob to enter Mom's rental house that day. Although I expected some of the usual trappings of disability, I was totally unprepared to the extent of Mom's decline. My collegiate activities had succeeded in dominating my mind and time; I hadn't considered that a person could debilitate so much in such a short time. There was no one to blame; it was just the nature of Mom's fight with MS. Yet as many can attest to, the pain of seeing her and the results of only a few months steady decline, were horrific.

The house smelled of stale cigarette smoke and held an eerie silence. In the distance could be heard the approaching metallic clatter of Mom's wheelchair and her constant emotional bantering with Dudley. Though

I did not know him as well as I should have, the love and care he had for my mom, his friend of 35 years, was clear. Purely platonic, Dudley's relationship with Gloria (my mother) had been mutually beneficial. She had a caring, knowledgeable, financially independent roommate that saw to her every need. In essence, Dudley became the big brother Mom never had. She became the needful and loving sister Dudley had never had. His stepsister, Katrina, had never been the kind of sibling he wanted. Their lifelong relationship had been the scene of many a turmoil. For Dudley, he finally had the opportunity to take care of someone else, rather than vice versa.

My arrival was greeted with emotionally charged excitement on Mom's part, and cool though friendly, indifference on Dudley's. Her appearance remains in my mind's eye to this day. My mother weighed less than ninety pounds. The wheelchair seemed to swallow her. Mom's limbs were mere twigs of flesh and bone incapable of providing the strength she needed to move about. Any small wind would break them into. The wrists of each hand were barely the diameter of a fifty cent piece. Her face, though amateurishly made up, was drawn and gaunt. She resembled a worn manikin on the way to discount. To make matters dramatically worse, her speech was severely broken and required endless practice for several minutes before she could actually complete a thought or sentence. This made me feel doubly uncomfortable because of my feebleness at comprehending her meaning. As I sit here now writing of the experience, I cannot even begin to fathom how uncomfortable *she* must have been, thinking that she was so horribly disfigured and so much more less a human being, for her own son to be afraid to visit. No doubt, she detected the fear in my eyes. How alone and full of overwhelming despair she must have felt. Yet she made every attempt to communicate and ease *my* pain. She struggled desperately with every word uttered. I, like so many, attempted to guess her next word, say it out loud, and then felt frustrated because it appeared I was doing more harm than good.

We sat at the kitchen table because it was time for her to eat. This ever humbling experience of feeding someone by hand shatters the "reality" of life. Such an act can dispel every thought you *knew* about *caring*. The experience is as close as I can describe to breathing life into another person. It's not the same as feeding a baby, for the baby knows not how and has never had the physical capabilities of feeding himself. Consider that the person was once vibrantly able to do life essential tasks such as breathing or defecating on his or her own. Now they *can't*. It would be eight years before I fully appreciated the significance of this experience.

Every single item was like mush or puréed as they say. Otherwise Mom would have had great difficulty eating. Over the years she had continued to sit and watch TV for hours while sucking on sugar enriched cough drops. That, coupled with her decreasing hand strength and lack of finger mobility which kept her from brushing her teeth resulted in a mouthful of cavities. Consequently, she had little ability to adequately chew her foods. The feeding process was long and tedious, or so I thought at the time. Is it not amazing how shallow we can be to want to just flee from the discomfort of seeing our loved ones physically deteriorate? Our feelings and discomforts should not matter in the slightest when one considers the alternative. None the less, sometimes it is hard to rise above our own selfish nature and truly give a damn. It is sad, but true! Adversity usually humbles you and hopefully makes one a better person. It did for me. Remembering this last day with my mom shall live with me for the rest of my life. The irony of how the "tables turned" on me several years later through my own similar adversity taught me that I should never take anything — especially love, family, and life itself — for granted.

After a late lunch for Mom, we adjourned to the den and attempted to hold a conversation. There was nothing striking in our exchange to mark the moment with the possible exception of my internal sadness and pity. I clearly remember my eagerness to flee the situation as quickly as possible, never once considering that this might be the last time I ever saw my mother alive again. Perhaps that is why this visit is so clear in my memory, because I have replayed it over and over a thousand times. Hardly two hours had passed when *my need* to leave urged me out the door. She had an unusual and most definite sadness in her eyes. Looking back, it is now clear to me that the look was one of longing for a happier and simpler time. Mom knew what I did not: we would never see each other again.

The Tuesday after Mother's Day was a normal spring day — sunny, bright, and airy. It seemed almost perfect. After completing my morning classes I was beginning to enjoy a mediocre lunch in the "Caf", or the Centenary dining hall, as we so casually referred to it. Seated with a couple of my fraternity brothers on the windowed West wall, nothing in my wildest nightmares could have prepared me for the events about to unfurl. Out of the corner of my eye I noticed a figure suddenly burst through the cafeteria's front door. It was Lea Volbine, secretary to the Dean of students. I thought nothing of it as she, like so many of the college staff, regularly dined with the students. However, she hurriedly moved along the endless line of waiting patrons as if looking for someone. This too seemed inconsequential for I assumed she was merrily hunting down Rick Anderson, her boss. She veered into the main dining area and began searching furiously. Glancing up I saw her speaking with a student pointing in our direction. As she approached our table her demeanor was solemn. This was my first indication that all was not well, for Mrs. Volbine was normally vibrant and cheery. As she approached closer, it became keenly aware to me that her determined line of sight was in my direction. Upon reaching me, she gave a quick fake smile and leaned in close to speak. "Tom, your grandfather just called and asked that you come immediately to their home." I asked, "What's wrong? Did he say?" She replied, "Something's happened! You need to go there now!" I ran the half a block to their home faster than I had ever run in my life while horrible thoughts jolted through my mind, but nothing could have prepared me for the truth.

Grandpa Campbell met me at the door as I was fumbling with the keys. I had never seen him in such utter despair. He was as pale as a ghost. His eyes were glassy and waterlogged as if he had been endlessly crying. To his left in the hallway was Earthaleen, the housekeeper for Mom and Dudley. "That's odd," I thought. Although she appeared so angelic, her hand covered her mouth and tears were streaming down her face. I knew that something horrific had happened. Yet even then, I had no idea it had anything to do with Mom. Grandpa put a hand on each shoulder, looked me in the eye and said, "Thomas come sit down, I need to tell you something." He could hardly speak and his hands upon my shoulders trembled uncontrollably. "What's happened?" I yelled. Then I realized Grandma was nowhere to be seen. I freaked and asked, "What's wrong?! Is Grandma okay?" Then he said the words I will never forget. "*She's* okay. *It's your mom*!" With that he lost all control, hugged me close, and let loose with a sea of tears. My next thought and physical urge was to charge out the door and run the seven blocks to Mom's house. In fact, it took all of Grandpa Campbell's urging and some of Earthaleen's considerable physical restraint to keep me from doing just that. They persuaded me to sit down. I was numb, yet still completely oblivious. Grandpa's sobbing words were slow and deliberate as he held my hands. "Something has happened at your mom's house. Grandma is there now and she insisted that you *not* come. She doesn't want you to have to deal with it." "What?" I pleaded. With that grandpa lost it and we hugged each other. His tears were contagious; I too began to cry without really knowing why. Suddenly the phone rang and Earthaleen answered it. It was Grandma. I rushed past Grandpa for the phone. As I put the receiver to my ear Earthaleen and Grandpa embraced and cried.

"Grandma this is Tom. What's happened?" She struggled to sound strong and supportive as always, yet her voice betrayed her. "Oh Thomas,

I am on my way back. Whatever you do, stay there; don't leave!" She abruptly disconnected. I turned to face the sobbing duo in the living room. My pleading expression must have said it all. They set me back on the sofa, each on one side. Earthaleen's arm was around my shoulders and Grandpa again took my hand. He began. Time stood still and my world shattered.

These are the facts as they were recounted to me that day. Earlier that morning Earthaleen had arrived at Mom and Dudley's to clean. Dudley met her at the door with a $100 bill in hand. He gave it to her and asked her to go buy him a carton of cigarettes. She did, and returned approximately 10 minutes later. Upon entering the house she felt uneasy because it was, as she said "unusually quiet." She noted that despite the ever running television there was not a sound to be heard. "It was deadly silent." Mom and Dudley were nowhere to be seen. She put her things down in the kitchen as usual. It was then that she noticed an unusual smell. She proceeded with the carton of Dudley's cigs through the den and down the long hallway. Stopping at Dudley's room, she called out to him. No reply. She turned towards Mom's room at the end of the hall and called out to her. No reply. She cautiously walked towards my mom's room only to be stopped cold by the site on the living room floor. There collapsed on his knees was Dudley. Bleeding profusely from an apparent self-inflicted gunshot to his head, Dudley was dead. She was horrified and screamed. She immediately turned to Mom's room and crept slowly forward. Entering the room she found my mom lying in her bed also dead from a similar gunshot to the head. She then called 911 and the Campbells.

By the time they had told me all of the details, Grandma Campbell was entering the front door. I turned and her face confirmed all that I had just heard. We rushed towards each other and embraced into a huddle of sobbing flesh. I don't remember the next several minutes, for the shock of it all was too much. It seemed like a horrible nightmare. In many ways, it still does.

In comparison, the next several hours seemed quite trivial. The Campbells were obviously devastated as well. In one fell swoop they had lost both of their best friends of thirty-five years. Their close friendship with Dudley Sumner and Gloria Ufert, my mom, had for the last five years become so intertwined. They were family. Not a day passed without at least a phone call between them. Every weekend found Dudley at Sunday dinner or the Campbells helping at Mom's. Joy and Charles Campbell, despite their personal strength were shell shocked. Though I had lost my mom, it was time for me to be a man of strength and action for them all. I don't remember thinking it or even questioning what needed to be done. Things just needed to be taken care of and for the first time in my life it was payback time. Looking back some twenty-six years later I realized that all of the years of growth and development culminated to this one juncture in time.

Details had to be arranged; family members needed to be notified; obituaries composed; funeral and burial arrangements set up; even legal questions addressed. It never occurred to me that others could handle these things. It just seemed I needed to be the "point man." All my life others had "taken care" of things. Now it was my turn.

It wasn't courageous. It was just what one had to do. In times of crisis, you don't always have time to think things through. Times like these, you have to go with your "gut" and that little inner voice that tries to lead you down the right path. The one example of this that clearly stands out dealt with the pastor of the Catholic parish my family, Ufert and Campbell, had attended all our lives. The pastor had called offering his condolences and rightly offered to perform the funeral services. Grandma Campbell disliked this man strongly. His presence at the services was more than she could bear. While all the "adults" were debating the issue in the living room that night, I snuck away and called him. I explained that due to the situation and the difficulties my grandmother had with him, it would be greatly appreciated if he would graciously allow us to ask another priest to take his place. He consented without debate and understood completely. God bless him for his compassion. I then returned to the living room and calmly announced that the issue had been dealt with and that our good friend Father Joe Reising would be performing Mom's services. In times of family despair and pain, one can't waste time bothering with petty differences. *Such trivialities need to just be dealt with as expeditiously and painlessly as possible. YOU DO WHAT YOU HAVE TO DO.*

Over the next several days friends, classmates, frat brothers, family members, teachers, even acquaintances called and dropped by offering endless comfort and friendship. Their love and concern consoled us all and came from as close as next door and even from across the nation. In spite of these offerings, only one single issue clouded an already horrific moment in our lives. Why? What could have possibly sparked this needless act of desperation? Although we will never know the cascading thoughts of hopeless despair that must have been bombarding Mom and Dudley's minds that morning, the coming days would reveal significant clues suggesting a probable cause for this horrible event.

Newspaper accounts of this family tragedy, while factual in content, seemed to imply a possible twist of romantic involvement. Nothing could have been farther from the truth. My first reaction was one of extreme indignation and outrage. How could anyone possibly have surmised such an accusation? I say accusation for that is how all the *living* parties involved received it. There was not a single soul who knew Gloria Ufert and Dudley Sumner that could accept such an explanation for this bizarre turn of events. Yet, for lack of a better reason it could be perceived as a logical conclusion. In today's world, perception is reality and such a perception was unthinkable in my mind. I could not live with this unsubstantiated version of my mom's death. A call was made to the local paper demanding a retraction, but without an alternative motive the report would stand.

Later that week an answer came, and from an unprejudiced source. The information that was given to Grandma Campbell fit perfectly considering the highly unusual nature of Mom's life. A friend of the family, we'll call her Mrs. Jenkins, telephoned to convey her condolences. As it happened she had been fully aware of Mom's situation for years because she worked for the local chapter of the Multiple Sclerosis Society. She had contacted Mom only five days prior to her death. As it turned out, my biological grandparents, Ira and Cleo Riley had made inquiries regarding appropriate local nursing home facilities for a patient with MS. Considering herself a friend, this individual had called Mom to ask if she was indeed considering such an option. Apparently, it took Mom by surprise as much as it had Mrs. Jenkins. For this reason she relayed the information to Mrs. Campbell; she knew what close friends Joy and Gloria had been. In addition the only other witness to this event, Dudley, was now deceased. Consequently during her conveyance of condolences, this friend asked if Grandma Campbell had been aware of this fact. She had not.

Before one draws any conclusions, allow me to offer the one that I have accepted. I shall go to my grave believing it and can accept no other explanation. Ira and Cleo Riley loved their daughter without question. They would have never done anything except what was best for Mom. Period! However, I believe Mom may have seen it differently. Consider her situation: she was totally disabled and completely dependent on others for her daily life. Yet the one shred of independence she possessed and continuously struggled to maintain, was her independent living arrangement on Merrick Street. MS, like so many crippling illnesses, affects the patient's psyche. Furthermore, there were few signs in her mind that her family, myself included, cared much. Her only son lived only a few blocks away and rarely visited. Her only daughter lived 1200 miles away and had begun a successful family life of her own. Her parents were elderly and could not sufficiently care for her needs. However, because they were her parents they had legal guardianship in the event of her physical/mental incapacity. It is extremely important to remember that for years Mom had distrusted the Rileys and felt tremendously paranoid about almost *everyone* around her. The disease had mentally affected her. Considering her state of mind when I saw her on Mother's Day, only two days prior to her death, she would have considered Nanny and Grandpa Riley's inquiries as a premeditated move to have her committed and placed in a nursing home. She would have misjudged their concern for treachery. Again, I believe that my grandparents had no such intentions. They were good caring people concerned for their daughter's welfare. Though for years I wrongly blamed them for Mom's death, maturity and hindsight have helped me clear them of any wrongdoing in my mind. This too, is another reason I chose to write this book.

Words, actions, and character clearly demonstrate two things: one, Dudley Sumner and Gloria Ufert were *not* romantically involved, just the best of friends; two, Ira and Cleo Riley *would have never* had their only daughter committed against her will and placed in a nursing home. They, as well as the rest of us, knew that Mom would have merely crawled up and died in such a place. In my opinion the Rileys were merely investigating the long term potential and probable cost of Mom's future convalescence. They wanted to make sure their only daughter was taken care of in their inevitable absence.

This begs the question of Dudley Sumner's involvement in Mom's death. Why? It is my opinion that following the Riley's inquiry, Mom felt trapped and had no further desire to continue living if it meant being placed in a nursing home. The Campbells and I firmly believed that she asked Dudley to put her out of her misery by committing an act of mercy. Dudley cared for Mom like no other friend. He saw and lived her misery and the suffering every single day for five years. He gave unselfishly to his friend of over thirty-five years. He also realized the futility of Mom's life in a nursing home. He and the Campbells thought nothing but the utmost care and love for Gloria Ufert as best friends should. However, for Dudley to have complied with Mom's request would have surely meant lifetime imprisonment or commitment to a psychiatric facility. Having been a free spirited Vietnam veteran, Dudley had been characterized by some as "odd". There were long periods of discord between him and his adopted stepsister over their inheritance as well as many other issues. I cannot help but believe that Dudley saw his act of mercy as a no way out dilemma. For the years he cared for my mom, Dudley could not have been happier. Consequently, for him to carry out my mom's desperate request would have meant the end of his happiness as he knew it.

Only days after their deaths, I met with my mom's lawyer to discuss her last will and testament. At that time he rightly advised me of the potential for a wrongful death suit against Dudley's estate. I was mortified that such a suggestion would even be made. There can be no doubt that I would have become a very rich young man. However, to me it would have been blood money and an admission that what Dudley did was wrong —*something I could never do.* I signed away all claims to that estate for wrongful death and have had no regrets. It can be argued that killing is wrong in any circumstance; however, in my heart and soul, I know that my mom is in a better place without suffering... and Dudley too. I have never blamed him or thought wrongly of his act of kindness, for I saw the true loving friendship he, my mom, and the Campbells had had over the years. To accuse him or anyone else for that matter, of causing my mom's death is ludicrous and unforgivable. Unfortunately, life is not kind and throws many obstacles in our way. We either accept them or change them into strengths. Everyone's level of tolerance for what life throws at us is different. Mom tolerated all that she could, and usually with a smile. Her strength and love have helped me survive life's slings and arrows. Dudley's undying friendship has certainly taught me the value of friends. I thank God for them both and the lessons they taught me.

Funerals and cemeteries are for the living, not the dead. For years I have always believed that my Irish ancestors had the right idea — a wake. Have the funeral, pay your respects, and pray to God for comfort.

Afterwards, throw a huge drunken party to celebrate the life of the departed and the glory of their eternal bliss with God in heaven. Life must go on and we should remember the smiles of our loved ones, not the decomposing heaps of their dead flesh. I believe that the soul is eternal and that is what we should hold dear. I do not need a gravesite to pray to my mom or to remember her by.

That, in my opinion is sick and depressing. We each deal with sadness in our own ways.

Therefore, if regularly visiting the grave sites of one's departed relations eases the pain, so be it. Just remember, they are not there. They are everywhere around us as guardian angels and nothing can imprison the eternal spirit God gives each of us. Rejoice in their smiles; celebrate the happiness they brought us while they lived; exalt the joyful memories of their lives. Please don't allow their funeral or gravesite to be the only lasting memory you have of the ones you have loved.

Perhaps death and funerals do have one unforeseen blessing — they can bring us closer together in the wake of our mutual loss. My sister Caru and I have never been closer than the moment when we held each other's hands kneeling in prayer at Mom's open casket. In that one moment all the past seemed to disappear. The week had been hard and demanding for me, but that one experience will forever be cherished in my memory of those caustic days.

The two memorial services were carried out with true professionalism by the mortuary service. It was immensely gratifying to see so many offer their respect for Mom and Dudley's memory. Caru and I had decided that the casket would be closed to the public. Though the morticians had been truly remarkable in their restoration of Mom's features, considering the nature of her death, I was mortified. That was not my mom. Through years of debilitation and the whole scale assault MS had berated upon her body, nothing compared to how fake and canvas-like she looked. That one experience spoke volumes to me about the frivolousness of human vanity. If ever I was in doubt of the value of cremation, morally or otherwise, my opinion changed with the site of my mom's dead body.

Likewise, the funerals themselves were performed beautifully and on cue. I say on cue because for me funerals seem so much like the last great performance of one's life. Sadly, society seems to place so much importance upon that performance rather than the person's life as a whole; if we would only spend so much time and money on making our *living* days as important as our days of dying. From the Tuesday of Mom's death until her funeral almost a week later, I did not cry. Too much needed to be done for time to be wasted on tears; however, once inside the limousine, I balled uncontrollably. It was my moment of relief and needed to be done. Anyone who says a man should not cry is just plain nuts! Crying is the body's way of releasing tension and distress. It is not that men should be taught not to cry. Rather we should focus more on the timing of that act. There is a time and place for all things we do. Crying has its place as well.

My good friend Dean Webster approached me after the funeral and offered the opportunity to get out and relax later that evening. I was reluctant at first but realized the need for letting go. He graciously agreed to have my girlfriend, Crystal, accompany us figuring her attendance might help as well. Oh, how wrong we would both be. The three of us went to one of our regular collegiate watering holes. Dean was determined that, after the past week's events I had deserved an evening of just letting go. He was the designated driver and all my beverages were covered. We had not anticipated the jealous nature of a drunken girlfriend.

An old neighborhood friend of mine, Suzanne, was also present at the bar. She and I had not seen each other in a number of years. She was nothing more than a comforting and consoling friend. However, my drunken girlfriend thought otherwise and mistook a gentlemanly request on my part as betrayal. I was feeling tired and tipsy. It was time for me to go home and go to bed. Dean was having a good time as well as my girlfriend. I did not want to disrupt their evening and asked Suzanne if she would make sure that my girlfriend made it safely back to her dormitory some 20 blocks away. Suzanne dizzily burst out loud, "you're going to leave your girlfriend here!?" Upon hearing this, Crystal jumped up and proceeded to walk back to the campus. Remembering my upbringing, I followed closely behind. It was okay for me to walk back to campus, but it would have been unthinkable to allow a young lady to do so by herself, especially in that neighborhood. During the entire walk back Crystal yelled and cursed at me in her drunken stupor. Once we arrived at the James dormitory, I explained that it had been a very long day for me; that we should just forget this ever happened, and go to sleep. I kissed her on the cheek, said good night, and walked away towards my grandparent's home across the street. I had not gotten 30 feet away when I heard Crystal scream and turned to see what was wrong. As I turned she rushed up, grabbed my wrist and slapped me across the face with her other hand. It took every ounce of self-control not to return the favor. Please don't get me wrong, I would never hit a woman; it's just against my nature and code of honor. However, considering that day's and the previous week's events, this act took me by complete surprise.

I slowly rubbed my face and looked her keenly in the eye. She could see the rage burning inside and I did notice a brief but apparent twinge of fear at what she had done. I took a deep breath and spoke the last words I have ever said to her since. "Crystal by morning you may very well have forgotten what you just did. Rest assured I will never forget for the rest of my life what you did to me on the night of my mother's funeral. I never want to see you again or even hear your name mentioned in my presence. Please don't ever speak to me again. Good night and goodbye." Some may say that I was harsh, but in my mind, it was unforgivable. For me there are three ultimate insults: first, flipping someone the "bird;" second, slapping them in the face; and third, spitting in their face. If I had been rude or mean, any one of those insults is well deserved and my conscience will tell me so. On this night I had been neither. It was an insult I could not bear and chose to deal with it in a way that demonstrated my intolerance of physical abuse and petty stupidity. Since then I have always maintained that if someone slaps me, they better have good reason, or our friendship, relationship, etc. is over then and there.

The weeks that followed were not memorable. My only desire was to get away from Shreveport and forget the whole damn thing. This chapter only demonstrates how impossible it is to forget something so traumatic in your life. It had taken four weeks to relive the horror and suffer the immeasurable depression at the holidays to write of this event so carefully "forgotten" for 26 years.

My entire book has been in limbo waiting to overcome this memory. Yet now as I finish this chapter, a great realization hits me hard. My life too, has been on hold trying to overcome what I started so many years ago. The experience has been uplifting and therapeutic. It only proves that we must stop trying to run away from our problems or sweeping them into the attic of our minds. They are still there and will continue to harangue us throughout our lives until we face them and deal with them. How can we possibly face new trials without finishing the old ones? Our past can be a guide to the future; however, it can also be our jailer. This chapter is meant to demonstrate again that the human spirit can overcome almost all obstacles. For those that we can't subdue right now are perhaps like a jigsaw puzzle; the answer lies within a series of experiences that when combined, provide clarity and reason in an otherwise dark and confused life.

Through the adversity of facing her illness and her death I see things and people a little more clearly.

For the first time in my life *death* literally paid a visit to *my* world. When *he* departed, Mom and Dudley went with him. This heart wrenching event in my life brought peace for my mom and an end to her suffering. Her death initiated my journey down several paths, each eventually leading me to a better place — self-reflection, closure and integrity. Nine years earlier she forfeited her parental rights so that I might have a better life. No doubt that it was unintentional, but in death she guaranteed her only son would come to terms with his own demons and give him the inspiration to conquer them.

It is my sincere hope and prayer that others may also be helped; that insight from my adversity may bring them peace and clarity to better deal with their own trials and tribulations.

10

NEVER SURRENDER

For weeks after Mom's death, I was plagued with guilt and endless questions regarding my lack of attention towards her as a dutiful son. I could not help but own some degree of responsibility in her death. Some days the depression would be so overwhelming that classes were skipped, old friends were avoided, and my only desire was to walk aimlessly with just my thoughts. Mrs. Campbell did her best to reassure me that my mom's death was in no way my fault. She repeatedly pointed out that I was still a young man trying to make his way in the world and that no one would blame me for wanting to avoid the daily reminder of Mom's debilitating illness. Even to this day I cannot help but ask, "what if I had put forth more effort in demonstrating my love for Mom?" Throughout our lives the little word "if" can loom so large. We question the decisions we've made, second guess the directions we've taken, and constantly beat ourselves up for the opportunities we've let pass us by. In the end we cannot snap our fingers and turn back the clock. Mistakes are only errors in judgment if we fail to learn from them. The primary lesson I learned from the entire ordeal of my mother's death can be summed up in a song by Corey Hart, "Never Surrender!"

"Just a little more time is all we're asking for
'cause just a little more time could open closin' doors.
Just a little uncertainty can bring you down.
And nobody wants to know you now,
And nobody wants to show you how.
So if you're lost and on your own,
You can never surrender.
And if your path won't lead you home
You can never surrender.
And when the night is cold and dark,
You can see, you can see light,
'cause no one can take away your right
To fight and to never surrender!"

Somehow a cassette copy of that song came into my possession shortly after her death. For the next several months I could be found listening to that song over and over and over to somehow connect with her. It became my life's theme song! I was convinced that Mom had lost all hope and could see no end to the suffering except through her death. In addition I finally recognized the real connection came with the realization she was now my champion guardian angel. I believe she inspires me to never surrender!

Over time I threw myself into my work, my studies, and my social life with a renewed sense of vitality. Within a year I was fortunate enough to be selected as a Lyndon Baines Johnson Congressional intern on Capitol Hill for Congressman Charles "Buddy" Roemer. It would be a full summer filled with work experience and travel. Chuck and Karen had moved to Erie, Pennsylvania, where Karen's family resided, in the hopes of breathing some fresh air into their lives. Furthermore, the fraternity was scheduled to have its national assembly in Atlanta, Georgia at the end of the summer. Therefore I saved what money I could for the arduous and expensive summer break. Unable to afford airfare I selected an All America Amtrak pass that would conveniently provide transportation to Washington, DC; Erie, Pennsylvania; Atlanta, Georgia; and then to New Orleans where I would catch a one way commuter flight home to Shreveport. Granted, the journey by train would take longer, but oh what a wonderful way to travel if you have the time.

The only problem with having long periods of time on your hands is that you tend to think too much. I distinctly remember thinking about Mom several times while traveling on Amtrak and hoping that someday I would make her proud; that in some way my successes would be worthy of all the sacrifice she had given for my benefit.

In between moments of melancholy and depressing thoughts of the recent past I was awestruck by the beauty of the American countryside. Coach fare meant that I basically spent all of my time seated or sleeping in an oversized chair. I always chose to sit in the window seat for the best possible view of the landscaping vistas that swept past as the passenger train sped me on my way to Washington. One fortunate luxury on the journey from Longview, Texas to Chicago, Illinois was the attachment of a sky car to our passenger caravan. Generally on long haul Amtrak junkets west of the Mississippi the rail company includes a unique double decker car with a glass ceiling that provides unbelievable views of the star studded night sky. When I was not in my seat or in the sky car, I spent my spare time conversing with other passengers in the club car. The entire trip to Washington DC was relaxing and offered a therapeutic period of self-reflection. By the time of my arrival in the nation's capital I felt revitalized and eager to fully experience my time inside "the Beltway."

Arriving at Union Station in early June of 1986 I somehow felt like Jimmy Stewart in "Mr. Smith Goes to Washington." For the 2 ½ months that I would be interning on Capitol Hill my residence was to be a dormitory on the campus of the American University. My dorm mate for the summer was a very amiable fellow named Fabio, an exchange student from Italy. The dorm was within walking distance to the nearest bus stop for the Metropolitan transit system. Monday through Friday I would traverse through the heart of Washington DC past Embassy Row at rush hour each morning and evening. My weekends were my own to tour the city and immerse myself in its rich culture.

I located Congressman Roemer's office in the Longworth Congressional House Office Building. My first day on the job was basically filled with the initial reintroduction to Buddy, intern orientation, staff introductions, and basic tours of the office itself and the grounds. The day seemed to fly by. In short, I quickly found my bearings and knew my way around all of the adjacent facilities, underground tunnel, and Capitol Hill itself within days. My duties were to assist the Congressman's paid staff members, help with constituent correspondence, research, and to some extent aid in the collaborative efforts of drafting reports and related legislation. The entire experience was exciting. Interning in a congressional office gave me a firsthand perspective on the inner workings of the legislative process. One quickly realizes that the majority of a Member's time is spent in committee. From the very first moment one steps into the inner sanctum of congressional affairs you are shell shocked by the incessant ringing of bells and the flashing of one or more colored light bulbs in the hallways. This is the congressional communication system that notifies Members and their staffs of the multitude of legislative activities such as roll calls, votes, opening and closing of committee hearings, etc. After the initial shock of discovering the underground tunnel and rail system between the various office buildings and "the Hill," the real awakening came during my visit as a spectator to the United States Senate. I eagerly anticipated witnessing some of the legendary great debates that are so portrayed as real and glorified in the lore of our American history. I was sadly disappointed! As I discovered the typical Senate oratories consist of a single United States Senator reading to a predominantly empty Senate chamber. The Senator's words are recorded by a chamber transcriber and typically only overheard by a small number of chamber staff and the odd number of gallery guests. It was a far cry from the colorful spectacle of Jimmy Stewart in Frank Capra's film. Nonetheless, my disappointment was short lived for I understood the impracticality of such drama in today's cumbersome Congressional schedule. For me the real enrichment of my soul came from the knowledge that, in some small way, I was helping improve the lives of others. Charles "Buddy" Roemer was and still is the most honest and dedicated public official I have ever had the honor of working for. Interning on his staff convinced me that public service was where God intended for my talents to be directed.

In my spare time I was most fortunate to have reconnected with a close fraternity brother, Greg Cooper, who happened to be working in DC for an environmental foundation. There were many weekends he and I would get together and tour the sites of which he was well acquainted because his father had retired from the military to live in nearby Virginia. On one such outing we went to the movies and saw "St. Elmo's Fire." A smash hit of the mid 1980s, this film had significant relevance for us both. It seemed that the characters were mirror images of our own circle of friends. Before the two of us departed from Washington, we had seen the movie four times. I was also very fortunate during my tenure in Washington to have reacquainted myself with a former political mentor. Morton B. had served as a special advisor to President Reagan and was considered one of the movers and shakers in the conservative movement of the Republican Party. I had previously met Morton while attending a state college Republican convention in Louisiana. I will never forget the one piece of advice he proffered to me when I asked him how to succeed in politics. He replied "if you want to succeed, in politics first become successful and well known at something else."

During that summer I attended a couple of the special youth campaign seminars his political foundation sponsored for the Republican youth movement. Morton's expertise taught me everything I needed to know about running youth campaigns, helping coordinate grassroots volunteer programs, maximizing public relations/media coverage, and how to effectively utilize your political opponents' weaknesses. We were well trained in the political tenet "Just because you're right doesn't mean you'll win," thereby stressing the importance of effective campaign organization.

Through my association with Morton I was honored to be invited to his annual Fourth of July festivities where I met some of the most influential politicos in the Republican Party. Ironically, one of the founding fathers of the conservative movement refused to shake my hand upon hearing for which Congressman I was interning. Apparently, Buddy had short circuited this individual's concerted efforts to force then speaker of the house Tip O'Neill into retirement. Though stunned by his obvious disgust for me and my employer I held my head high and lost immediate respect for him. As far as I was concerned, regardless of this individual's influence and power, his disdain for Buddy Roemer would not dismantle my respect or esteem for my political idol.

On a more positive note Morton did provide me with a rare opportunity to gain a new perspective on a historical landmark. I and several other participants in his foundation's workshop accompanied Morton on an inner tubing expedition down the Potomac River past Harpers Ferry, Virginia. That experience, as well as my tours of Mount Vernon, the Washington/Lincoln/Jefferson Memorials, and nearly 40 hours combined touring the Smithsonian museums provided me with an up close and personal feel for the legends of American history. My summer in Washington only deepened my love and appreciation for this great nation we call home.

In mid-August I hopped aboard Amtrak once again and made my way to Erie via New York City and Philadelphia. My one and only experience in the Big Apple was fast and furious. Arriving at Grand Central Station I had less than 40 min. to commute eight city blocks to New York Penn Station — in rush hour traffic! Rushing to the taxi stand with my luggage in tow I managed to grab a cab driven by a Romanian cabbie. Flashing a $50 bill in his face I explained the rush to make my connection. In a dash we were off. He made the trip with roughly 10 min. to spare, at one point having to navigate the traffic by partially driving over the curb and barely missing a pedestrian! Early the next morning I arrived in Erie to spend a week with my folks and catch my breath.

Chuck and Karen's new home was a quaint little house in the heart of Erie proper. The neighborhood consisted of almost zero lot lines bunched together to create the image of a stereotypical postwar urban setting. The two-story was deceptively larger than it appeared including a basement washer/dryer area. Although my stay would be short, it provided the opportunity to catch up with the folks and spend some time with Karen's family all of whom I had not seen in a number of years. The two distinct memories I have of that trip "home" both involved an air of tension between Chuck and me. The first was his sarcastic remark about the number of dress shirts I had hung to iron for repacking.

He was aghast that someone my age could possibly need so many. I tried to explain they were all necessary due to the nature of my summer long trip, but it was an act of futility. The other incident revolved around the CSPAN coverage of the Iran/Contra hearings. In a condescending tone, Chuck remarked, "See what your president has done!" I took a deep breath and calmly retorted "Dad, you're not even registered to vote! So frankly you've got no right to bitch." I found out later from Karen that my point stung Chuck so deeply he went out and registered the week after I left. Although I took Chuck's animosity personally it would be several years later before I discovered that he was only lashing out to cover for his injured pride at having to rely on his wife and in-laws so far away from home.

It took over two days of travel from Erie to Atlanta, Georgia to attend my fraternity's national assembly. None the less, the inspirational bonding of brotherhood that was experienced during that week was well worth the trip. My first Sinfonian convention cemented lifelong friendships and confirmed I had chosen the right fraternity. Our contingent from Louisiana, a.k.a. province 14, was nicknamed from thereafter as the Louisiana Mafia. Under the skilled leadership of our CPR (college province representative) Brian S., "The Godfather," and our PG (province governor) Rory T. we canvassed and lobbied the voting delegates to secure passage of constitutional legislation that would maintain the status of our professional fraternity as all male. The weeklong festivities included numerous concerts, sightseeing, legislative sessions, serenading various females throughout the hotel and city, and a great deal of boisterous beer drinking. After that first national assembly, I was a confirmed lifelong Sinfonian. The train trip home was aboard Amtrak's Southern Crescent special to New Orleans. From there I flew home to Shreveport. It had been a whirlwind summer and I was exhausted.

The revelry of such a successful summer had dramatically helped me overcome my depressing thoughts of the previous spring. Arriving back at Centenary in time for the coming semester I was in good spirits. Although it was impossible to erase the horrible memories of the events surrounding Mom's death, my summer travels had successfully filled me with eagerness to profit from my experiences. I dove into the new academic year with renewed vigor.

My junior year at Centenary brought an increased caseload both academically and socially. I was beginning my third year of studies in political science and history which meant more in depth and increasingly difficult classes. So far I was maintaining an A average in my degree plan while working thirty-five hours a week. In addition, I continued my editorship of the college newspaper, had been successfully elected chapter president of the Eta Upsilon chapter of the fraternity, intensified my activities with College Republicans to become a collegiate representative on the state party's central committee, and even volunteered occasionally as a driver/chaperone for my former high schools out of town debate trips. To say the least, my life was full and spare time didn't exist. Rest assured I did make time for my social life which was further enhanced by the opening of a restaurant/bar directly across the street from my dormitory. This establishment became my second home. Regardless of how full my schedule was, I always made time to spend a couple of hours with the Campbells for Sunday dinner. In college one learns very quickly never to turn down free food especially if it's home cooked by your grandma!

My spiritual life took somewhat of a backseat on my list of priorities. Raised a Roman Catholic I still felt at home with the church though my attendance to mass was becoming more and more infrequent. One of my coworkers, Brad, at Portland's, was the son of a preacher. On several occasions, after a sleepover at his place following a Friday or Saturday night bar hop, I would accompany him in his search to find the right spiritual congregation. We attended services for the denominations of Southern Baptist, Pentecostal, Methodist, Presbyterian, and others. Though I felt comfortable and welcome within each house of God none made me feel at home like that of my childhood parish at St. John Berchman's. Placing a greater emphasis on my civic responsibilities, academic affairs, and indeed my social pleasures resulted in a gradual withdrawal from my childhood faith. Regular attendance to church became increasingly less important. Though I became less and less of a "church goer," my faith in God and the spiritual connection to His divine essence never faltered. Increasingly, I became less religious but more spiritual in my faith. Though I had been a Eucharistic minister while in high school and considered myself a fairly devout Catholic; my gradual withdrawal from the church, and organized religions in general began during my collegiate years. This issue is important to mention to set the stage for life events that began to occur shortly after I graduated from college. The point is, that though my faith in and association with religious institutions diminished, my spiritual connection to God and His eternal love were strengthened by the adversities life threw in my way. No religious building had sustained me through my troubles. Yet, I felt God's presence. In fact, I firmly believe that it was my faith in God, my mom's sacrifices, and the strong family foundations given to me by the Campbells that provided me with the determination and sheer will to survive. In my case however, overcompensation became the norm and seriously jeopardized my future.

During my third year in college I made a monumental decision to room by myself. After two years of rooming with Rob, the need for my own private space superseded all considerations of friendship and financial practicality. Though he was not pleased with my decision, Rob certainly understood. My lack of privacy became paramount shortly after being humorously embarrassed when he walked in and interrupted me with my girlfriend in mid-intercourse. She didn't find it funny at all, and I must admit deep seated personal desires made the need for privacy and discretion essential. Furthermore, my increased volunteer work with various political campaigns and my newfound responsibilities as the fraternity's college province representative forced me to seek more space to accommodate the files and materials associated with this increased workload.

My activities with College Republicans (CRs) dramatically increased because of requests for campaign volunteers from the state Republican Party. I and my fellow CRs helped with electing a Republican successor to Buddy Roemer's seat after he retired. We were the driving force to select a particular candidate for the party's nomination — a decision in hindsight I deeply regret. The individual, thanks to the enthusiastic poignant questioning of his rivals by our college members, handily won the nomination. He was eventually elected to the congressional seat which he held until his retirement over 20 years later. Though fairly reliable rumors surfaced during the campaign and throughout his tenure in Congress regarding his sexual orientation (these allegations were reported in detail during a Showtime movie special about the negative effect of key "closeted" political figures), the congressman had a very successful marriage and raised a family. His voting record was regarded as one of the most vitriolic antigay positions in Congress. For a short period of time I worked as a constituency aid in his district office until I was suddenly dismissed due to "budget constraints." Grandma Campbell never forgave him for my dismissal and always claimed it was due to his subconscious fears of being accused for being a hypocrite. I must admit working for a United States Congressman provided me with great experience. Being able to pick up the telephone, dial anywhere in the nation and solve a constituent's problem simply because of who I worked for, was very self-satisfying. For me that was the quintessential definition of public service.

Following the successful election of the congressman, our college Republican chapter leaped into action once again to support a Republican congressman from South Louisiana running for the United States Senate. Our chapter was one of the leading forces to coordinate a statewide youth campaign seeking to elect the first Republican senator from Louisiana in nearly a century. Though our efforts were unsuccessful the experience did provide me personally with some extraordinary benefits. I was introduced to and became acquainted with many influential Republicans in and out of the state. My hard work and enthusiasm earned me a position on the state staff hosting the 1988 Republican national convention in New Orleans. My responsibilities at the convention primarily consisted of allocating and carefully doling out the state party's allotment of convention floor tickets. This position brought me into direct contact with senior party officials from across the nation as well as key campaign staffers for the

Bush/Quayle presidential campaign. At one point I was provided a VIP pass to the senior campaign staff townhouse in the French Quarter. This was a reciprocal thank you gift for guaranteeing prime seating on the convention floor to staffers during Bush's acceptance speech. Due to this and other special privileges I was much honored to have met party celebrities like Arnold Schwarzenegger and Charlton Heston.

During my spare time I took full advantage of my position to fully experience the carnival atmosphere of a political party national convention. In addition, I was able to fully enjoy the more "touristy" and social benefits that give New Orleans its dual reputation for a city that never sleeps and the nickname "sin city." Although the city was cleaner than ever before, at least according to residents, some of my personal activities could hardly be considered clean. On a couple of occasions, with a paranoid sense of adventure, I traversed some of the more seedy avenues of the French quarter in search of pleasurable satisfaction. I am highly ashamed of my behavior because it was severely hypocritical of me to be publicly supporting a staunchly antigay political platform, while secretly slithering in darkness to fulfill my natural born desires. In many ways my vigorous defense of the GOP's "core family values" was in essence a desperate attempt to convince myself and others of something I was not — straight! It would be three years before I admitted to myself this simple fact of my life.

Over the remaining two years of my college career both the social and academic spheres of my world would be chaotic. My fourth year in college was without a doubt the most difficult academically. It was absolutely devastating to my academic average. In a few of the courses required for my degree, I struggled to maintain acceptable passing grades. It is difficult to say what the real source of my trouble was. It could have been my internal turmoil over my sexual identity which resulted in more frequent risky adventures. Or it could have been simply a case of collegiate burnout. Regardless of the cause my increased partying and drinking certainly contributed to my academic decline. Weekend after weekend I would spend dancing long hours at Club Capri followed more and more frequently by visits to homosexual and bisexual hangouts. Naturally all of this nightlife involved serious alcohol consumption. At the same time I was desperately striving to maintain a charade of the All American straight boy. In hindsight I'm not sure how many people I fooled, but I certainly was able to foolishly convince myself.

My claim to fame of having supported myself and financing my college education came with a heavy price; namely, a self-destructive behavior that nearly cost me my family, my academic career and possibly my life. By the end of five years at Centenary my alcoholic binges resulted in a less than stellar academic record coupled with a reckless and somewhat unsafe social life of numerous inebriated one night stands. These included both the heterosexual and homosexual variety. While still claiming to be "straight," and firmly believing that I was, my frequent ventures into the homosexual lifestyle were kept as discrete and camouflaged as possible. I was able to fool many, myself included, that these adventures were merely the result of weakened defenses brought on by the influence of alcohol. At times my personal life involved simultaneous "committed" heterosexual relationships while secretly pursuing the "fun and games" of a "closeted" gay double life, or "on the down low" as it is sometimes referred to.

My secret adventures into the gay world brought me in contact with previously unknown "party favors" that opened a whole new world of potential addiction. In addition to my regular consumption of alcohol, these frequent homosexual encounters introduced me to sexually exhilarating inhalers known as "poppers" (alkyl nitrates, discreetly known as video head cleaner). While my particular personal experience with these and other "liberating" inducers revolved around the homosexual community, it should not be prejudiced or stereotyped as strictly occurring in just the "gay" world. On the contrary, many of the same drugs are regularly utilized in and around the heterosexual social world as well. For many people, both gay and straight, drugs of many forms are a regular "mood stimulator" or "defense inhibitor." Regardless, all of these drugs are dangerous, illegal, and physically detrimental.

I distinctly remember a very poignant conversation with Karen. We were discussing my obvious preference for alcohol during my college years. She asked rather nonchalantly, "why do you drink?" After carefully considering my response for a few moments, I remarked, "I think it's because for a few hours you can feel good and forget your problems." She sighed and responded with the profound wisdom of an experienced adult, "That doesn't make any sense! Your problems are still there when you wake up the next morning." My only answer to her was that for a brief moment in time one can "just forget about it for a while." Though at the time we did not see eye to eye on the subject her words of wisdom were dead on right. Unfortunately, for so many people a brief lapse of comprehension seems far more preferable than facing the truth and dealing with their problems head on. For several years to come I would be just such a person willing to take great risks rather than meeting my adversity directly and facing the consequences for better or worse.

By the time that I graduated in 1988, my walk down the aisle was a far cry from my previous successes in grade school and high school. I received no outstanding awards or marks of notoriety for my academic success. I simply graduated without honors and received my double degree in political science and history barely accomplishing a high B average. (I would like to offer a deep personal note of thanks to the outstanding members of the Centenary College administration and academic staff. My five years at Centenary offered me the great honor and privilege of knowing and being instructed by outstanding academics such as Dr. Rodney Grunes, Dr. Earl Labor, Dr. Donald Webb, Dr. Alton Hancock, and Dr. Sam Sheppard among others). Although Chuck was unable to attend Karen, Joy, and Charles did.

I was less than proud of my mediocre success. The eyes of my family demonstrated a similar appraisal.

Following graduation I could no longer live on campus. That summer I and two fraternity brothers agreed to rent a slightly shabby duplex apartment. Having lived by myself for the last couple of years I had become accustomed to a neater and tidy atmosphere than my frat brothers. Consequently our roommate arrangement didn't last long. I tried futilely for a couple of months to afford the place by myself. However, my extracurricular social activities forced an end to my independent living situation. Though I was working full time I could not make ends meet, primarily due to the endless drinking and partying that I continued to pursue. I partied on as if I were still in college while attempting to maintain my job and perform numerous community and political services. My participation in artistic and political organizations throughout the community created a perceived obligation to dress appropriately to fit the part. Such fashionable attire requires money. My entire situation was financially unbearable. I could not afford to live on my own any longer.

My only saving graces were Joy and Charles Campbell. I and the family had come to terms midway through my college years and compromises were reached that seemed to heal old wounds with regards to my drinking. Therefore, a rather innocuous situation of "don't ask don't tell" was the status quo. As long as my drinking caused no harm, did not interfere with my responsibilities at work or home, and caused no disparaging embarrassment, my social life was my own business. My constrained cash flow, coupled with a lack of suitable stable roommates, forced me to move in with the Campbell's. The situation of having to live with my grandparents was somewhat humiliating, at least from my perspective. The truth of the matter was that I was damned lucky they put up with my "BS" for as long as they did! Furthermore, they argued that it was a reasonable arrangement because recent events required that I should save as much money as I could. It is by the sheer grace of God and the Campbell's inexhaustible loving patience that I didn't wind up in jail or dead. The most notable example of this fact was that through divine intervention and a significant degree of Mrs. Campbell's influence I was awarded a Rotary international Fellowship to study in Australia. Joy Campbell's boss fervently recommended my fellowship application to his Rotary club. Thank you Dr. P! That same year my political mentor Morton B nominated me to receive a highly prestigious White House Fellowship. Considering the lackluster result of my college career and my mischievous social behavior, this was far more than I deserved! God truly works in mysterious ways.

For years my residency with Grandma and Grandpa Campbell would be jokingly referred to as "life at the nursing home!" The entire experience was a strain on us all. I tried desperately to continue my social life of partying and drinking, frequently trying to sneak in late at night without awakening the "old folks." In the end my excessive drinking caught up with me. God bless Joy and Charles for their endless patience and intestinal fortitude; however, even they reached a point of no return the morning I was discovered passed out on their front doorstep. From that moment on my drinking and flagrant disrespect for them and their home would no longer be tolerated. Within a week I began a feeble adventure to seek help through Alcoholics Anonymous (AA).

From the outset my personal feelings about attending AA were dread and absolute embarrassment. I have no doubt that these same fears are pretty common among initiates to any 12 step program that requires an internal admission a problem really does exist. You have to admit to yourself and others you have a problem. That alone is a major step in dealing with addiction. Furthermore, the embarrassment of coming to terms with an addiction problem, of any kind, was monumental for someone so committed to maintaining a public persona of being an ideal role model. How could this happen to me? I was a scholarship recipient, honor student from grade school and high school, well respected among my peers and adults alike for my community activities, hardworking young man that earned a double bachelor's degree while working nearly full time. Until five years before, I had never had a drink in my life. If nothing else, AA helped me understand that not only was I an alcoholic, but that I was also an alcoholic child of an alcoholic, my mom. The group therapy sessions brought back into stark reality memories of my mom's regular beer drinking and popping of prescription pills. Furthermore, Alcoholics Anonymous stresses that while genetic traits play a vital role in an individual's addictive personality one cannot excuse the behavior by simply blaming the parents. We make our own decisions and are the creators of our own destiny. AA's 12 step program was an excellent character building experience because it stresses acceptance of your faults, atonement for your errors, building of self-esteem, forgiveness for human frailty, faith in God, and a realization that real solutions are never quick fixes. In many ways this program was another step in *adversity building character.*

For four months I regularly attended a weekly session of AA. Unfortunately, I ended the experience abruptly because of a rather dramatic encounter. For nearly 2 hours on the last night of my AA treatment I became deeply engrossed in a revealing conversation with a fellow alcoholic. After our meeting he and I were engaged in a deep discussion of life events and mutually similar addictive behavior. Over sodas and coffee we spent the time relegating how alcohol had affected our lives. This alternating conversation helped me realize that I was not alone in my affliction and poignantly confirmed that alcoholism, like any addiction, is a daily struggle. However, his final revelation struck me like a ton of bricks; to cope with his alcoholism he attended an AA meeting every single day! Reflecting on this point I realized that many of our group's attendees seemed to have simply transferred their addiction for alcohol to an addiction for AA meetings. For them it didn't seem that therapy was working. Granted, these individuals' lives were no longer being devastated by alcohol, but they had become so dependent on the meetings, they weren't living — they were existing.

Alcoholics Anonymous is a wonderful program that has helped thousands if not millions of people. For whatever reason, it just didn't work well for me. In all probability my psyche wasn't ready to completely admit I had a problem and commit to the regimen. AA did at least help me confront the strong probability of a drinking problem and resulted in a significant decline in my drinking habit. One must remember my mom had just passed away, I was preparing for a long overseas adventure, and my ego had suffered the humility of being forced to reside with my grandparents to financially survive. I just wasn't ready to stop feeling some euphoria that drinking and barhopping deceptively seemed to provide. In addition, about this time, I unexpectedly lost my job at Portland's due to a false accusation of theft. Years later I would come to find out that I was made a scapegoat by a coworker who in all probability was the actual thief. By the grace of God and through the patient generosity of the Campbells I was able to struggle through until my departure for Australia in early February of 1989. Before long, alcohol would be the least of my troubles.

11   LOVE LOST, ME FOUND

As FAR AS I was concerned, the choice between my two fellowship nominations was an easy one — Australia! Anticipating a future career in politics, I concluded that further opportunities to work in the White House would present themselves. Financially speaking, it was a no brainer. The Rotary Fellowship was an all-expense paid trip for one year abroad including airfare, room and board, tuition, books, and miscellaneous sundries. The White House Fellowship was for a shorter period of time and allocated a mere stipend of $900 a month to cover my living expenses. Last, but certainly not least, was the fact that I weighed the realistic expectations of ever being able to travel to a foreign country and study at one of the top universities in my field all expenses paid, ever again — versus the probable opportunity of returning to Washington DC in the future to work for less money for an indeterminate amount of time. Opportunity was knocking with an Aussie accent and I answered the door!

After careful consideration it became unrealistic and unjust to quickly par down all of my travels and experiences while in Australia into a single chapter. Therefore, I have decided to provide a detailed compilation of my year abroad into a second book entitled, "ABC; A SECOND HOME" (ABC standing for Australia Beyond Canberra). I have already suggested to a few of my Aussie friends a tentative layout for the contents of this work. It shall include photos and personal thoughts from several Australian friends describing their hometowns and the cultural highlights that make their part of Australia an integral part of the world "Down Under." It will also include my own personal thoughts and observations of the people and locales that I was fortunate to experience.

*   *   *   *

My return to the States carried a mixed bag of emotions. The 10 months "Down Under" were extremely rewarding. My studies in East Asian political affairs definitely provided a beneficial base of knowledge for preparing to enter graduate school. Having completed a nearly fifty page thesis on the Chinese influences of samurai education in the Tokugawa period of Japanese history, I easily proved my abilities to fulfill the necessary research requirements at the graduate level. Furthermore, coupled with my previous acquisitions of recommendations from respected experts/practitioners in the fields of political science and history, my time in Australia provided even more such authorities to support my grad school application.

Having completed my Rotary Fellowship it was impossible to extend my student visa. Unable to stay but equally unwilling to ask the only woman I ever loved, an Aussie, to abandon her family, her studies, or her homeland I came home with a heavy heart. For weeks she and I telephoned each other expressing our love and dedication, but deep down I hoped she would follow my advice by dating others to confirm if our relationship was meant to be. As is so often the case when you give advice, reality slaps you in the face and it hurts far worse than you expected. Several months later I was completely devastated when Jenney informed me of her new boyfriend. Deep down I knew this day would come but it hurt still the same. Over time I came to realize it was the best for both of us but she will always remain my first true love.

I've said it many times; the only thing Aussies do fast is get off work at five 'o'clock and head for the nearest pub. That of course is an exaggeration; however, they do like to drink. Thanks to Alcoholics Anonymous, my drinking had curtailed somewhat, but Australia is certainly not the place to try and quit cold turkey. Back home, during my college days, downing a six pack of beer was not a difficult task. My first night "down under" taught me all I needed to know about the alcohol content of the average Australian beer. Whereas in the United States the percentage was roughly 4 ½%, in Australia it was nearly double. After five Fosters lagers I had to be carried out of the pub. During my 10 months Australian adventure there were numerous occasions when I "fell off the wagon". By the time I had returned to the states my tolerance level, though certainly not as high as it had been in college, was markedly higher than when I left. Before long, alcohol would be the least of my troubles.

While I had been away in Australia, another blow to my future plans came unexpectedly. Chuck and Karen had gotten a divorce. This devastating news was conveyed very nonchalantly in a simple letter from Chuck that depressed me for weeks. I was 15,000 miles away and could do nothing. This sudden turn of events immediately raised doubts as to the future of my graduate school plans at the University of Kentucky in Lexington. Shortly before my departure abroad, a visit with them in Lexington brought great promise to the idea of residing at home while studying international relations at UK. Such an arrangement had been discussed and all parties concerned supported the idea as financially pragmatic. I spent a week with Karen shortly after my return home. It was a wonderful visit but she made clear that living at home would have to be temporary until I was able to find employment and a place of my own. She was not completely sure that she would remain in Lexington and felt that the securing of my own residence would be best. This greatly disappointed me, but I completely understood. To say the least my hopes of attending grad school at UK were completely undermined, at least temporarily. Any hope of further pursuing the idea required a sizable amount of cash to finance relocation, securing a residence, and obtaining employment. I would have to go to work and save like crazy!

Throughout life we make plans for the future and are constantly amazed when they fall short of our expectations. A friend of mine once said "life is what happens when you have other things planned!" My hopes of attending graduate school while living comfortably in the safety nest at home to save on my personal expenses had been dashed unexpectedly by my own parents. Though not their fault, Chuck and Karen's marital tragedy directly affected my personal and professional life. To have relied so heavily on the easy comfort of "life at home with the folks" was a miscalculation of monumental proportion. Parents are supposed to help their children "stand on their own two feet," but after that their responsibilities, except for love and advice, really *do* end. I believe another key lesson adversity teaches us is that you must adapt to ever changing circumstances and strive to become self-reliant.

Previous experience had already confirmed that living with my grandparents would eventually end in disaster. Fortunately an old friend and coworker from Portland's solved that dilemma, though he had an ulterior motive in mind. Jesse's kindness and generosity were sincere but I had no idea that secretly he was in love with me. Living with his sister and niece in a three bedroom townhouse Jesse made arrangements for me to move in and stay as long as was necessary. Initially, he moved into his niece's room while she shared her mother's. After a few weeks I felt extremely guilty that my presence and the resulting disruption of their household were unacceptable. Therefore, I innocently insisted that there was no difficulty in sharing a room with Jesse thereby allowing for a return to their previous living arrangements. Having roomed with another guy numerous times before, I saw no problem with this setup. However, this time would be different. My previous roommate situations had always involved separate beds; Jesse and I would be sharing a bed. At first nothing was out of the ordinary — just two guys sleeping in the same bed. After a few nights all of that changed.

It came as a complete surprise. There had been rumors over the years that Jesse was gay but I had dismissed them as simply conjecture because of his artistic and somewhat effeminate demeanor. From my perspective, after all the years of rumor and slander towards myself, I naïvely gave Jesse the same benefit of the doubt and made no stereotypical assumptions that the rumors were true. However, a few nights after we began sharing the same room and bed, confirmation of those rumors hit like a lightning bolt. In the middle of the night Jessie put the moves on me which I immediately rebuked and out of friendship graciously ignored. A few nights later he made his advances again. This time I accepted. The pain and hurt of my breakup with Jenney in addition to the overwhelming surge of secret desires that I had denied for years combined to accommodate the awakening of a lifetime. Past experiences had been spontaneous and certainly questionable due to the influence of alcohol. However, this time neither of those factors were involved. I gave in of my own free will and for the first time felt no shame or guilt. It was as if a heavy burden had been lifted from my shoulders.

For months we carried on a secret and very discreet physical relationship. For me however, it was a simple case of two friends having fun and helping each other out — not so for Jesse. I carried on feeling no sense of obligation or attachment. Gradually over time, with the previous inhibition of shame or guilt no longer restraining me, I began to wander and seek out additional partners for my sexual pleasure. This behavior was both dangerous and insensitive to the situation that had developed with Jesse. Selfishly, I saw no problem with it. In fact I was completely shocked when he confronted me with feelings of hurt and rejection at my apparent lack of mutual affection. Our friendship and living arrangement quickly soured.

During this time my need for financial solvency drove me to seeking employment wherever I could find it. Initially my prospects had been bleak. Upon my return from Australia all five employment agencies in the Shreveport area had determined that I was overqualified for any positions they had available. By sheer luck I landed a retail sales position as a clerk selling lady shoes for Dillards department store. The job rapidly became menial and tedious perpetuating a growing sense of underachievement. At the same time I was also performing duties simultaneously as a tutor and groundskeeper for one of Grandma Campbell's closest friends. Her grandson was in need of organization and study skills that I was able to provide. Furthermore, her sizable corner lot grounds required regular maintenance. Though my dual responsibilities provided access to free transportation and a generous income, when combined with my full time position at Dillards, I was left with no days off. A year of this strenuous pace made me irritable and eager to seek alternate arrangements. Regularly I broke the monotony of working three jobs by house sitting for numerous friends to help build up my savings.

Being over employed, however, created stress and frustration that only magnified my need for outlets of release. I sought these by keeping up a regular social life and "burning the candle at both ends." My time at Dillards brought a new acquaintance into my life that happened to share some of the same social pastimes. His name was Brandon. We had met through a mutual acquaintance that worked in the same mini mall where my Dillards outlet was located. Over time we continued to see each other socially and developed an extremely close physical relationship. For the first time in my life I freely fell in love with another man.

Brandon Allister Jones was a whimsical and charming older man. Approximately five feet eleven inches tall, with dark short curly hair,

Brandon initially approached and clearly indicated his affections for me. Though not seeking any long term committed relationship, I was struck by his genuine feelings and my ego was captivated that an obviously successful older fellow desired *me*. Our initial "get together" was the most intense I had yet experienced, but the development of our relationship led me in a direction I never anticipated.

As I have mentioned, shortly after my return home I came to grips with the fact that I was, and evidently had always been, gay. Naturally this awakening helped ease the return to some of my previous haunts — the gay bar scene. This deceptive sense of freedom only intensified my quest for "good times." Within a year of my return, I had wandered down a dangerous road of risky behavior. While still making every effort to maintain a "straight" image, my long held resistance to other "party favors" crumbled. Seduced by the combination of finally accepting my nature and the freedom of finally allowing myself to fall in love with another man, basically shattered every rationalization I had falsely created to protect my career. Unfortunately the individual I had fallen in love with had a significantly more "liberal" perspective on recreational drugs, as did his best friend.

Until that time, my staunch refusal to "partake" in the recreational use of marijuana had been solely based on my desire to respond honestly with a profound "NO" if and when the question was raised by the voters considering me for public office. In the light of peer pressure, my position was easily supported by the fact that the practice is illegal. The allure of sexual euphoria and the protection of absolute secrecy between consenting adults behind closed doors made resistance seemingly pointless.

I thank God for the sheer graciousness of His love. I can point to no other reason that adequately explains how I did not wind up arrested or dead. In many ways my life experience perfectly supports the claim that marijuana is merely a "gateway" to other more insidious and extremely deadly drugs. Over the next several years my "trip" down this self-destructive path would lead me to become intimately acquainted with pot, cocaine, and crack. It would cost me nearly everything; two wonderful and meaningful relationships, several friendships, my self-respect, and nearly even my life. In the end, *Addiction does Bear Consequences*. Earlier I quoted a Japanese proverb that suggests how an addiction like alcohol, drugs, or even sex starts so casually or recreationally. Over time, even a short amount of time, it transforms from a casual occurrence into a life altering adversity. Failure to recognize its life consuming detriments can be catastrophic. In addition, it is indeed an adversity that cannot be conquered without help and support; foolish pride deceives the heart and mind from asking for help. As with all adversity in life its defeat is a common cause and victory over it is a testament to the human spirit.

By late 1990 Brandon was also becoming frustrated with his employment situation and the small town atmosphere of Shreveport. Together we began to make plans for relocating to a larger more cosmopolitan community. To carefully prepare my family and friends for the eventual shock of moving I had skillfully contrived a web of lies to camouflage my relationship. As far as they all knew I was dating a recently divorced wealthy woman named Barbara. This conveniently explained my regular absences from gatherings and my frequent appearances driving a strange automobile. The storyline I created about moving out of town hinged solely on the premise that a friend of Barbara's had offered to share his two bedroom apartment with me in Dallas, Texas. The stage was set and we moved in February of 1991.

My relationship with Brandon resulted in two major personal accomplishments. First, I found a partner to provide the ways and means of escaping my dead end life in Shreveport. Second, by introducing me to the Oak Lawn area of Dallas on a couple of trips to scout for apartments, Brandon had opened my eyes to a completely unknown world. Here I discovered a "safe" and promising community where homosexuality was acceptable and livable. In Oak Lawn I witnessed an entire community of shops, restaurants, bars, and apartments where gay men and women walked freely hand in hand living unobstructed lives. Up until that awakening I had thought such a community only existed in San Francisco.

We found a very comfortable large scale apartment complex in a Dallas suburb known as Irving, Texas. I immediately started my search for employment. As a certified LVN, Brandon had no difficulty finding a job. For me it took nearly 6 weeks, but eventually I was fortunate enough to gain employment as a restaurant cashier at a nearby airport Holiday Inn. An eager learner with strong "people skills," I took to the position easily. Within six months I was offered the position of assistant food and beverage manager and a significant increase in pay. I absolutely loved the job. The hours were long and the responsibilities numerous, but for the first time in a very long time I was challenged and felt my talents were being utilized. My boss was an excellent teacher and the Holiday Inn was an ideal training ground for dealing with the public.

At the outset, life with Brandon in Irving was successful. We both were working and enjoying creating a comfortable home life while frequently enjoying the benefits of being able to share a committed gay relationship. Over time our work schedules evolved into a routine of work and sleep. Both of us were working long hours consistently from two or three in the afternoon to well past midnight. My commute time to work was 10 to 15 minutes. Brandon however, because he was working for a nursing agency, was spending anywhere from an hour to an hour and a half traveling from hospital to hospital with no set routine. Though our scheduled hours were similar, our days off and time to spend together varied greatly. In fact, our mutual days off rarely occurred more than once or twice a month. This increasingly became a burden and helped to exacerbate a growing rift in our relationship.

Like my "mentor" of so many years before, Brandon was 15 years my senior. Furthermore, over time the vigorous physical aspects of our relationship had begun to wane. In all honesty, as a newcomer to the more open and relaxed atmosphere of the gay culture I had discovered in Oak Lawn, my keen desires to enjoy and explore the social nightlife overwhelmed any sense of dedication and loyalty. I was bound and determined to find and develop friendships with others of my own age. This was neither a problem nor a concern for Brandon who trusted in my commitment to monogamy implicitly. Traditionally, in relationships between significantly older and younger partners, regardless of sexual orientation, the motivating drives for satisfaction and fulfillment can be strikingly at odds. The older partner who has already enjoyed and tasted the varieties of life is generally content to pursue a more settled lifestyle. In contrast the younger partner tends to seek the more socialized and vibrant nightlife of bars and partying. In most cases this ultimately results in a failed relationship. For me an unsatisfied and generally unfulfilled sexual libido was prey to the lure of uncommitted and anonymous physical encounters. The stereotypical "love had nothing to do with it" rationalization seemed to easily dismiss any and all feelings of guilt or remorse. Furthermore, Brandon's increasingly diminished interest in physical love only further reinforced my lack of commitment to love and loyalty. Grandma Campbell always used to say, "If you're not getting it at home, you'll go out and find it somewhere else." Her cynical appraisal was by no means a vote of approval but rather a harsh statement of reality. There is no doubt in my mind that Brandon and I loved each other deeply. However, my obsession and addiction to sex were definitely the sources of our relationship failure.

To compound the lack of physical intimacy between us, drug and alcohol addiction played a heavy role. On no occasion of my infidelity was alcohol or some form of addictive drug agent, such as marijuana or cocaine, not involved. It must be understood that prior to my relationship with Brandon, and association with some of his close friends, I had never been exposed to or used either of these recreational drugs. Though the introduction and ready access to these items was made fully available to me by these individuals, they are in no way to blame for my decision to partake. A key component in society's failing war on drugs is a lack of personal responsibility. Therefore, I take full responsibility for my actions and the consequences thereof.

Perhaps adversity is God's method of "hard love." As I have said before no one promised that life would be easy — *it's not*. If we go through life always blaming others for our own mishaps then that is taking the easy way out never having to pay our fair share for the privilege. Eventually that self-deceiving line of thinking will backfire and explode in your face forcing one to come to terms with decisions that you and you alone, are responsible for. God gave man the freedom of choice. Other than life itself it is perhaps His greatest gift to us all. In the end we must choose to do what is right or wrong, but we should be neither surprised nor angry about the consequences of our own actions.

12

I'M STILL STANDING AND ROLLING ON

CRASH! MY FIRST thought was "damn that hurt!" Then a series of questions flooded my hazy consciousness. It was about 5:15 A.M. and I was almost finished with my, now routine, morning jog.

During the latter years of college I had attempted to improve my physical well-being through running, tennis, and some weightlifting. It was partly due to a lifelong desire to be a popular jock and partly from a natural realization at twenty that I did have some decent physical attributes. This keen desire to work out had a lot to do with the company I kept — mostly the guys on our college soccer team. They were the "in" party crowd on campus and had the girls coming from all directions. Naturally, I concluded that working out and hanging around the team would make me equally popular thereby attracting my share of the babes. It is funny one doesn't realize until many years later, none of that really matters. People either like you for who you are or they don't, no matter what you do. In the end, why be something you're not for people who don't really care in the first place. I now exercise because I want to for me, not to impress someone else.

The first of the "big three", as I like to call them, started with a crash, then several more over time. It wasn't until seven years later in August of 1992 that many things came together to paint a clear picture of what was happening to me. There were numerous "accidents" while jogging in the early morning. I just "blew it off." Either I wasn't fully awake, or not paying attention; never anything more serious than that. While in high school there had been what the doctors called, after 10 days of extensive tests, a "spinal virus." Don't ask me! I still don't know what that means. All I do know is that it left me unable to walk for two weeks and it disappeared as mysteriously as it had appeared. I had fallen off a ladder onto my back only the year before. Fortunately, there had been no damage other than my pride. The wind had been knocked out of me but x-rays revealed no skeletal or muscular damage. For two days during my sophomore year in college I had neuralgia of the eye. When you're young and carefree, nothing seems to faze you even if your vision is blindingly cloudy for no apparent reason. After it passed, I just went on as if nothing had happened. It wasn't until two years later that I learned a doctor had foretold my future, warning my family of its undeniable connections to a certain disease, MS.

Another series of clues developed in 1989 while I was studying in Australia. Since tennis was the only sport I had ever been halfway decent at, I tried to play regularly. My "uni-mate" Andrew Stinson was quite good. His talents were far superior to mine and I had little hope of defeating him when we decided to play in April. Our warm up was uneventful, the air was breezy yet typically warm for Canberra in early fall (because Australia is below the equator, their seasons are reversed). After weeks of jibes and feather ruffling Andrew and I were both eager to play. In the middle of the first set, it began. Gradually through the second set it continued to plague me. My left foot and leg were dragging. Andrew could definitely see that something was wrong. We had already become good friends and he graciously offered to postpone the match until another day. Naturally, my male ego and pride were challenged, so I continued to play futilely. From that day forth, no matter how hard I tried, no matter how hard I exercised, no matter how hard I played, I just couldn't do it. My conclusion was something muscular must be wrong; it would eventually heal and then disappear. Coming from a medical family, *I of course knew better than anyone what to do with regards to my own body*, right!? Not! It was the first time in many years I had felt the fear of being incomplete. Being basically a nerd in high school, and certainly not one of the jocks I so admired, my efforts were concentrated on academics in an attempt to overcome my "adversity." It had certainly paid off with scholarships to college and now a full expense paid fellowship to study abroad. Yet that confidence was shaken by the fear of being unable to physically accomplish my goals — of becoming a fertile and athletic young man — what society teaches every guy to strive to be. Society says "If you don't, then you're not a 'real man'." After my return to the States and then my relocation to Texas, the struggle to ignore my homosexual desires and this continuing physical setback were only additional blows to my masculinity. As so many stubborn people do, I decided to ignore these problems in the hope that they would just go away.

Adversity brings coincidence!? That is what I thought years later. It was Mother's Day 1992. This was a big day at the hotel, at least in the restaurant. A huge buffet was planned in the hopes that we would generate business on an otherwise dead weekend for the Holiday Inn. I was the Assistant Food and Beverage Director. In other words, I had spent weeks planning and coordinating the event under Richard Osprey's direction. He was the Food & Beverage (F&B) Director and had spent the last year teaching me everything about the hotel F&B industry. I worked my ass off and loved every minute of my job. It wasn't uncommon for me to put in 12 or 16 hours a shift. My regular duties included managing the bar and restaurant during the lunch and dinner hours, inventory control, daily liquor ordering, employee relations, and scheduling, In addition, as junior management I had direct contact with the public and was responsible for making our guests as comfortable as possible. Basically Richard delegated to me the responsibilities he either hated or wasn't quite adept at. I was on my feet all day long. I never loved a job more. Mother's Day 1992, was just such a day, but even more so.

Anticipating the "church crowd," we scheduled our brunch buffet to begin at 11:00 AM and continue through till 2:00 PM. In addition, we had advertised dinner specials for that evening. To say the least, it was a busy day. There were numerous times I felt weak and needed to sit down. Again I thought nothing of it and simply excused my fatigue for having worked so hard putting the buffet plans together. Yet by the end of the day around 6:00 PM I could not walk! If you think that was scary, just imagine driving my Honda Civic home; it was a standard stick shift with clutch! Here's a clue; if you can't use your legs to walk, give up trying to drive a standard!

I took several days off to "recuperate." During that time I thought a soak in the apartment complex hot tub might help. Wrong! After soaking and relaxing in the hot bubbling water for about 30 min., I couldn't get out! There was no one around to help and the heat was becoming unbearable. Today our modern society jokes about the TV commercial for medical lifelines: "Help me! I've fallen and can't reach my beer!"

Until you have suddenly lost the ability to independently move yourself physically out of a dangerous situation, you will never know true fear. To go from the realm of complete physical independence to that murky chasm of physical uncertainty in a split second is horrifying. The human mind does one of two things, usually simultaneously: first, we panic; then we use analytical reasoning to get us out of the predicament we are in. Trust me, I freaked! I was a fairly muscular, adept young man. *How was this possible? What was happening to me? Why was this happening to me? What have I done to deserve this?* All of these thoughts clouded my thinking, until reality kicked me in the butt: *I needed to get out of there before things turned for the worse.* Ever see that school biology film showing how prehistoric creatures first emerged from the sea onto dry land? They literally dragged themselves from the water by their forearms or "fins." That evening I could have been a stunt double for that prehistoric fish. I could not use my legs at all! They were fully extended and would not retract to offer me any standing leverage out of the hot tub. In addition my leg muscles felt completely out of energy and control; that heat was exhausting. Even after I had extracted myself from that boiling cauldron, it took an additional thirty minutes before I was strong enough to stand and stagger home. The entire ordeal was unnerving. Yet one final act was still required before I submitted to seeing a doctor. Sometimes people can be the dumbest creatures on earth!

After a good night's sleep I awoke feeling weak yet refreshed and up to par. I spent several minutes explaining the previous night adventure to my other half, Brandon.

Naturally as a nurse, he was concerned. I merrily shrugged off the incident as yet another example of overworking myself. He suggested a nice cool dip in the pool. That sounded like a great idea. Granted, I had to walk slowly because since the Mother's Day fiasco my rapid gait had not yet returned. Again I surmised that I was working too hard. Brandon helped me walk the half a block to the pool. The steps were a bit of a struggle, but we finally made it. As I stepped down into the pool a strange sensation hit me. It was confusing and frightening. Suddenly my body was shocked to experience a simultaneous difference in "feelings." While my right leg and foot "felt" cool, my left "felt" no temperature sensation at all. It was as if my left leg and foot were too insulated to register any sensation at all. Again my mind freaked. I was scared — ignoring this problem was no longer an option. My fear came from not knowing what was happening. Over the years many adversities had come my way and were decimated by faith in God and myself. Now faith *in me* was in question.

After a few days of inquiries, Brandon had obtained the name of a highly recommended neurologist in Plano, Texas. An appointment was made. My lover was very comforting and did his best to ease my fears. Deep down I was frightened because this problem was out of my control and certainly capable of placing me in a similar situation to that of my mom so many years before. That memory weighed heavily on my mind as we met the good doctor. After an extensive examination of my legs and feet he suggested an MRI. Magnetic Resonance Imaging he explained was far more advanced than its earlier counterpart, the CT scan. Doctors were actually able to see detailed three dimensional pictures of organs and their frailties. He noted that such advancement would make diagnosis of my problem easier and potentially more successful to treat.

I informed Richard at work of the progress in determining my ailment. He and the entire hotel staff were supportive. However, Richard was highly concerned for my professional well-being. He noted that my condition, should it continue would jeopardize my career in F & B. It would be impossible to fulfill my duties if medical restrictions prohibited me from being on my feet for long periods of time. Furthermore he noted that the company's health insurance would not provide complete coverage. At his suggestion I met with his girlfriend, Carla. She worked for an insurance company that might be interested in hiring me. Carla and I had met several times and she was very supportive of my endeavors at the hotel. A former hotel staff member herself, she valued and appreciated my people skills as well as my organizational abilities. She had spoken, on my behalf, with her superior. Carla inquired if the company, Sister's Insurance (SIC), would have an opening suited to my ongoing physical condition. Namely, was an office position available that could provide regular hours, 9 to 5, Monday through Friday? God truly works in mysterious ways! SIC did have such a position;

they were interested in me; and they would pay me three thousand dollars more than I was making now. More importantly, being an insurance company, they offered far better health coverage than the hotel, requiring only a one year pre-existing exclusion for my present illness. I was both excited and saddened by this turn of fate.

For two weeks I agonized over the decision and was so stressed that large clumps of hair fell from my head. I loved the daily contact with the public and thoroughly enjoyed the management responsibility entrusted to me. It was clear however, that this was too good an opportunity to pass up. The general manager of my hotel called to see me. Kees Elderer was a fine man and a true gentleman. He understood my situation but hated to lose me as an employee. His offer to keep me on staff was more than generous and superseded the company's regular pay increase by 2%. In addition he offered to transfer me to a position that would accommodate the need for a change in hours and responsibilities. I was in awe of his generosity. In the end however, my choice was clear: I would have to accept Carla's offer; it was far too good to pass up. To my relief, clumps of hair did not continue to fall! It was the smartest decision of my life, yet I wouldn't appreciate how much for another 90 days.

The first MRI scanned the lumbar region of my spinal column — nothing. The scan revealed absolutely no abnormalities. So a second MRI was arranged and scanned the cervical section of my spine. It also revealed nothing out of the ordinary.

By this time I had already begun my new position at Sister Insurance Company and was very pleased — completely bored, but pleased. It was a far cry from my duties at the Holiday Inn. I had no contact with the public and spent eight hours performing the menial task of accounting data input. I say menial because for a "people person" like me, data entry held few challenges and offered even fewer rewarding experiences to better serve my fellow man. It was a fine job but not well suited to my talents.

A third MRI was performed in August of 1992. Eureka! They found something. I was so relieved to now have actual proof of a brain! The truth of the matter was that not only had they found my brain, but also a "hotspot" on its right side. Doctors can be really vague when they explain a "hotspot." Basically it's a diseased area of the brain. To properly diagnose the "hotspot" would require analysis of the brain matter or what they call "gray matter" from the spine. I never got that far. However, the attending radiologist noted, from years of experience reading such scans that in his professional opinion the "hotspot" appeared to be the beginning stages of multiple sclerosis, or MS.

My first "big one" was a heavy blow. Yet, I was comforted. Much research and advances in treatment had occurred since Mom's diagnosis over a decade earlier. I had seen what giving up can do and how important one's mental outlook, or as the Germans would say "Weltanschauung", was to treatment and recovery. In many ways I felt that out of respect and honor for my mom there was no question but to endure and overcome. It was the way she would want me to be. There was also a deep impression that Mom's experience had, in many ways, prepared me for this kind of hardship. *In that respect I thank God for both adversities, Mom's and mine.*

*   *   *   *

Adversity *does* bring challenges! September 28, 1992 was mine — certainly not my first and by no means my last. I was in the wrong place, at the wrong time, with the wrong person, for the wrong reason. Thank God there were more of the right people in my life than the other. The next chapter is dedicated to them.

Brandon and I had started the evening with an argument. Not so much a fight as an ongoing disagreement over our relationship. Without a doubt, he was the most loving and dedicated person I had ever been involved with, but I didn't know it. That isn't to say other people were less loving or dedicated, because each gave what they could. Either I was too immature or things were just not right. In hindsight I can honestly say that I wasn't ready or willing to accept what they had to offer. Furthermore, I was probably too selfish and self-consumed to realize what I had staring me in the face. That was certainly the case with Brandon. As in so many cases throughout our lives we just spin our wheels looking for something we're too blind to see.

I was leading a double life "in the closet". Immediately upon my return from abroad reality "cold cocked" me — I was gay. This was a major surprise for me. It wasn't that I hadn't been having homosexual relations before now. However, I *had* fallen madly in love with a beautiful Aussie girl while in her homeland. Up to that point I had just rationalized my gay activities as just getting my "rocks off." For some reason it was easier and less complicated with guys than it had ever been with girls. At least that was what I kept telling myself. I had "sown my oats" enough in college and those experiences successfully fooled me and many others into thinking I was "straight" just like all my friends.

Upon my return to the states, a close personal friend helped reality slap me in the face. Though my friend was deeply "closeted" himself, our friendship combined with his undying generosity, brought about an unexpected result. I finally admitted to myself that I was gay. Trust me, it's hard not to when you're having sex with him in his bed, all the while professing deep sorrow over the loss of the one woman you ever truly loved. Who's kidding who? After several months of what I considered just being "buddies," I met Brandon. Granted it was one of my drunken stupors that brought us together, but it was my first admittance of loving a man for something other than just sex. I must admit now that sex is what caused 9/28/92 to happen. Rather, I should say my obsession with sex is what caused 9/28/92. You see that is why I was out at 3:30 AM and not at home where I should have been. I should have heeded the old saying, "if you're not in bed by one o'clock, you should be at home asleep." That is a bit shallow to say, but at the time, it would have served me well. Thank God Brandon was a better man than I.

13

REHABILATATION FOR MY BODY AND SOUL

*ADVERSITY BUILDS CHARACTER…*WITHIN one month adversity had hit me broadside like a ton of bricks. Not only was I diagnosed with probable multiple sclerosis, but now due to my own stupidity and lecherous desires I had suffered a spinal fracture. Specifically, my doctors referred to it as an incomplete fracture of the fifth and sixth cervical vertebrae. In the process, my lover of two years now probably suspected me of infidelity and the lies to my family about my true lifestyle were bound to be discovered. Adversity was forcing me to face my own character flaws and atone for them. Building character is not always an easy or personally desirable course of action. Yet in the end when each of us is forced to face our true character, we can only hope and pray it is a portrait that we are proud of. The truth is that because of these adversities I had become a better person. Yet I still didn't know it… adversity had another strike to throw my way.

After two days in ICU and another four in managed care, the rehabilitation process began. As I've said before, God works in mysterious ways – I know this to be true. To complicate my already difficult physical rehab situation, a second blood test analysis confirmed my HIV status. Dealing with the healing process of an incomplete spinal fracture complicated by the intricacies of additional neuromuscular problems from MS can be dealt with tangibly. Coping with the stigma and the unknown effects that would undoubtedly develop from the virus that leads eventually to AIDS was almost more than I could bear. In addition, my concern for Brandon's health only added further stress to the rapidly deteriorating situation. It would be one thing to have contracted HIV myself because of my deplorable behavior, but a completely unforgivable act to have infected another as a result of my infidelity. That was a crime that I would never be able to forgive myself for having committed. Thank God that was not the case, or so Brandon told me. For whatever reason, he refused to get tested for the virus, arguing that it was not a burden he wanted to face at the time. His primary concern was my recovery. God bless him for that! Years later when we met for the last time Brandon would confess that he never wanted to be tested because in a weird way it was comforting not to know; as he put it, never to have to worry about having sex ever again. I remember at that time thinking to myself how petty it seemed because I didn't have that luxury. He probably said it because of the pain and broken heart he was coping with over our breakup. That's another story that will come later.

The day I woke up with a sudden change of heart and a renewed sense of purpose can only be explained as an act of God. Having seen what happens when the human spirit gives up, in my mom's case — an overpowering sense of hopelessness, was not going to happen to me... The drive, the determination, and the sheer will to live could not have been possible without my faith in God and the loving encouragement of Brandon and all of the medical personnel at PRH. That bastion of support girded me for the physical and mental struggle rehabilitation was going to require. Knowing now that the HIV virus was streaming through my veins instilled in me the mental, physical, and emotional drive to overcome those physical challenges I could conquer. In essence my thought process concluded that it would be impossible to survive the effects of HIV if I did not first master my new physical challenges.

Physical rehabilitation is no easy task. Furthermore, learning how to cope with physical challenges does not come readily. In fact it is a long arduous process of trial and error, measured in a seemingly endless cycle of success and failure. Rehab of any kind does not come quickly and literally tears at the very fabric of your soul. I am living proof however, that in God's infinite creative wisdom there is no greater miracle than the adaptive and ever healing human mind and body. I was most fortunate to have been given rare insight into this rehabilitative process by the individuals most closely associated with my care: my physical therapist, occupational therapist, my personal nurse, and my recreational/pool therapist. Their thoughtful and inspiring dedication to my recovery was invaluable to my positive mental outlook. The encouragement I received from these miracle workers of modern medicine made the difference between self-pity and the sheer will power to overcome my adversity. For example, the staff at PRH was enthusiastically supportive when I chose to comically decorate my titanium halo for the Halloween and Christmas holidays. Furthermore, my efforts to spread humor and good cheer to my fellow patients by regularly surprising the nursing staff with my wheelchair horn were met with smiles rather than frowns. Herein lays a prime example of the incredible healing power of a strong positive mental outlook. In many ways my successful recovery was similar to the philosophy of actor Robin Williams in the movie *Patch Adams*: You must treat the patient, not just the illness. However, the gathering of such a collaborative team spirit did not come overnight.

My first physical therapist was a relatively young girl who was both dedicated and blindly determined. However, her "bedside manner" left a lot to be desired! For the first six weeks of my therapy even the basic task of getting out of bed and into a wheelchair was exhausting. The extra twenty-seven pounds of metal screwed into my skull made every movement precarious. Physical therapy requires several different routines of exercise to rebuild stamina and balance. Primarily the patient exercises on a padded table referred to as an exercise mat. One of the exercises that are initially attempted is simply to sit on the side of the table with your legs hanging over the edge and your feet on the floor. Daily routines call for a series of bends at the waist with your arms outstretched to help orient your body for stability. Normally for a "partially paralyzed" patient this is a fatiguing endeavor. My situation was exacerbated by the additional weight upon my head which completely made orientation and equilibrium nearly impossible. My PT became increasingly impatient and condescending towards my fears of toppling over onto the floor. Granted every precaution was taken by the therapist and her assistant to ensure that this did not occur. However, insurance and guarantees never totally erase fears of the unknown. Under normal circumstances such exercises were understandably difficult and tedious, but my titanium halo only magnified the strain. At one point my PT lost her patience and said in an accusatory tone, "I am sick and tired of blaming the halo for your resistance to the necessary exercises of your recovery!" For me that was the straw that broke the camel's back. The very next day I requested to meet with my entire therapy team at the end of the week to voice my concerns. At that meeting I strongly expressed my desire to change therapists, arguing politely that the present arrangement was counterproductive. I requested another PT who had shown great interest and compassion for my condition. Over time our conversations had been enlightening and reassuring that she was more capable of producing results while acknowledging my limitations.

If there is one lesson that I learned from years of listening to Chuck and Karen tell stories from their work at the hospital, it was that patients needed to be their own advocates. As the healthcare profession has grown, patients have increasingly become mere case numbers and charts of endless statistics. Medical personnel are overworked and hospitals are understaffed resulting in a dehumanizing effect on the profession as a whole. No one is at fault. It is just the simple truth about our modern healthcare industry. Therefore, patients and their families must be vigilant and proactive to prevent improper care, careless mistakes, and a desensitizing approach to medical treatment. I am eternally grateful to Chuck and Karen for teaching me to be my own advocate!

Personal advocacy requires a personal responsibility. This means one must take the initiative to be well informed and educated about your own health and treatment. Such a direct approach to your own health and well-being does not condone rudeness or blind arrogance in the face of expert medical opinion; it does require an honest self-appraisal of your medical condition. Therefore, you and you alone must have the mental wherewithal to take care of yourself and a positive attitude in your recovery. There are centuries of historical examples demonstrating the miraculous healing power of the mind over the body. With the right support and encouragement, a strong positive outlook can literally turn disasters into miracles. I'm living proof of that fact.

My new physical therapist (PT), Layne, proceeded to teach me more about my own body than I ever knew before. By way of her instruction and suggestion, I discovered that the human body can adapt remarkably to permanent injury. She taught me how to utilize "spastic energy" caused by my MS as a means to overcome irreversible neurological damage to the spine. She was patient and supportive, all the while being determined and persistent in our daily physical therapy. Her methods were creative and open minded to alternatives such as biofeedback in a constant effort to help my body adapt to its new life altering condition. Many of these previously nontraditional methods required coordinated assistance from other members of my therapy team.

One of the advantages of the team model approach to rehabilitative care is that every aspect of the patient's therapy is carefully integrated. Meeting weekly each member of the team is able to update their colleagues about the specific developments in their sphere of the therapy. This routine intercommunication perfectly enhances joint cooperation for the patient's total care. For example, my PT was able to provide relevant medical evidence to my social worker showing the therapeutic benefits of biofeedback that justified its insurance coverage. Similarly, thanks to the coordinated progress reports and projected cost benefit analysis of both physical and occupational therapy my insurance carrier approved the purchase of both manual and electric wheelchairs. Traditionally, insurance will cover one or the other but never both! Remarkably my therapy team's magnificent group effort successfully garnered over one quarter of a million dollars in benefit coverage. Repeatedly the PRH therapy staff stressed that it was their job to secure every possible benefit so that I could focus on recovery.

For 5 ½ months I resided at Plano Rehab progressing steadily towards discharge and my return home. During that period of time my strength and stamina steadily improved. Due to the excellent dietary care I easily recovered the nearly twenty-five pounds that had been lost following the accident, embarrassingly gaining nearly six waist sizes by the end of my inpatient status. Shortly before my discharge in early 1993, the titanium metal halo was removed to reveal the miraculous healing of my spinal fracture. However, one of the metal screws did weaken and become loose just after Christmas. I have never felt more intense pain in my life. This experience did require massive amounts of pain relievers to endure the agony. Though I do not recall much of the week long ordeal, I have been told that the medicated induced euphoria resulted in my ironic observations of three humorous clichés; one, that it was absolutely true — *I had holes in my head*; two, that *I really did have a screw loose*; and three, *I had finally lost my halo*! Laughter heals the world.

Careful attention was also given to the goal of my successful reintegration into life after rehab. For example, one week before my discharge, I resided independently in a preparatory "apartment" without supervision for a full twenty-four hours. This therapy technique helps the patient cope mentally, physically, emotionally and psychologically with the rigors of returning home. Though medical assistance was only an emergency button away with periodic spot checks to insure my safety, I was solely responsible for dressing myself, bathing, meal preparation, independent transfers from my wheelchair to the bed and toilet. The experience was terrifying, but essential for a successful reintegration into "normal life." My occupational therapist (OT) and social worker cooperated closely with the Texas Rehabilitation Commission (TRC) to ensure the acquisition of necessary equipment required for independent living and my return to work. Their joint efforts provided adaptive computer equipment and a fully equipped handicapped van that predominately insured a successful return home.

I would be remiss if I did not properly recognize the invaluable service of both my doctor and my employer. Dr. R expertly coordinated every aspect of my rehabilitative therapy. His expert care and deeply compassionate demeanor made the difference between success and failure in my recovery. As for my employer, Mr. H. at Sister Insurance Company Inc. was no less than a miracle worker. His generosity and heartfelt concern were endless. In fact had it not been for a direct phone call personally to the CEO of the insurance carrier, I probably would not have been fully covered. As it turned out, a policy technicality would have prevented full coverage for my injuries and medical care. However, because of Mr. H's financial holdings as a major stockholder in the insurance carrier, his wishes carried a great deal of weight. I learned later that he had instructed the carrier that "I was to be fully covered without any questions."

All of this support and encouragement from my therapy staff, employer, co-workers and friends greatly enhanced the recuperative process. That core support group would have been inherently inhibited were it not for the further blessings of understanding, forgiveness and unconditional love from my "adopted" family. Words cannot adequately describe the shame and humility I felt at the moment of confession to the Campbell clan. In one fell swoop they discovered the extent of my physical injuries, the depth of deception I had contrived to conceal my lifestyle, and the overwhelming sense of final doom with the announcement of my HIV status. Their eyes conveyed disappointment, but their hearts demonstrated true love. So many afflicted with HIV never know such compassion. I will be forever humbled in the light of such a divine blessing.

Finally I have to express the deepest amount of love, respect, and admiration for Brandon. Throughout this entire ordeal he continued to work full time at Plano Rehab striving to fulfill his employment obligations for the hospital while simultaneously keeping tabs on my therapy and recovery. Despite any hidden feelings of hurt or anger he demonstrated an unquestionable loving devotion towards me. The daily anguish of watching me struggle through my rigorous rehab regimen must have been doubly grueling for him because he would then have to go home to an empty apartment. The undeniable cause for my injuries, my infidelity, must have been like a dagger driven into his back right through his heart. However, his overwhelming love seemed to give him reason enough for forgiveness. He never offered any words of complaint, though fatigue and stress were clearly visible in his eyes and upon his face. I am deeply grateful for his love and he will always hold a special place in my heart.

In the end, my life, my recovery, and everything I am since September 28, 1992 are living proof that miracles happen every day. Furthermore, your life can change in a split second, but through the grace of God and the love and friendship of people in your life you can overcome any hardship. Accepting that reality unquestionably leads me to know in my heart and soul that *Adversity Builds Character*. None of these accomplishments would have been possible without the dedicated love and friendship of all these remarkable people. Their determination to help me succeed is deeply humbling and only further demonstrates the incredible healing power of another person's faith in your character. I thank God for their belief in me, for it has made me a better person.

*   *   *   *

My recovery had been no less than miraculous. Initially the prognosis had been bleak. However, after the morning that I woke up in my PRH bed and was able to wiggle the right big toe the amount of "physical return" gradually increased. On the day of my admission into PRH I could barely move my right forearm. 5 ½ months later, with the exception of full triceps muscular control, I was able to fully extend and retract both of my arms. Swelling in the spinal column had caused the loss of fine motor skills in both hands resulting in the inability to independently extend seven of my ten fingers. However, through the diligent and expert training from my therapy staff, I learned how to retain my full grasp and grip in the hands. Though the sensory perception of touch and feel was slightly diminished in my fingertips, lower legs, and feet I was still able to distinguish relatively well between hot and cold temperatures, as well as sharp and dull sensations. I recovered full bowel and bladder control making the need for internal catheters no longer essential. In fact enough physical recovery was accomplished to make normal sexual functionality possible. To demonstrate the miraculous nature of my recovery it must be noted that approximately only 8% of patients with my type of spinal cord injury have any degree of return. Thank you God!

Following my discharge, I continued physical rehab therapy as an outpatient for the next 2 ½ years. Within ten months I was able to return to work at Sisters Insurance, Inc. on a part time basis that eventually progressed to full time within another year. Thanks to the hard work of my social worker and my TRC caseworker, the acquisition of my fully equipped handicap van made independent transportation possible. Their guidance and outstanding counseling gave me great insight into the confusing quagmire of government assistance for the physically challenged. That alone is a gift that keeps on giving for which I can never possibly repay. By the end of my outpatient therapy, Dr. R. was astounded at the degree of my rehabilitation. Though I could not walk primarily due to a side effect of MS known as foot drop, the ability to fully extend and partially retract my legs was achieved. I could independently roll and if necessary crawl. Thanks to the excellent forethought of Leslie, my occupational therapist, I learned how to dress myself from another patient who had achieved complete independence from her physical challenges. Assistive durable medical equipment such as a bath bench and toilet seat was now routine essentials in my life. Thanks to the excellent rehab training I had received, my ability to transfer myself to and from the wheelchair by means of lifting and sliding was as easy as "normal" physical functions. Rehab taught me how to carefully consider a problem, assess the necessary solution, and adapt accordingly. I could no longer run and jump, but I could certainly "roll" with the best of them!

For several years following my accident and discharge from rehab I still required significant assistance at home. It would be a few years before my physical abilities would adapt sufficiently to allow for the safe and effective physicality to cook, bathe, and perform other daily functions. For most of this period I was blessed to have the loving and competent assistance of my state funded home health aide named Peggy K. She was truly an angel sent from God. Though my traditional rehab therapy through the hospital ended, I managed to participate in hippo therapy (horseback riding) at the Rocky Top Therapeutic Riding Center. Every Saturday for two years I received some of the most beneficial rehab therapy of my entire recovery. Horseback riding is extremely therapeutic because your lower body performs nearly normal muscular functions thanks to the bodily movements of the horse you are straddling. That therapeutic pastime would be one I would have continued for the rest of my life had I been able to afford to do so.

For the next several years remarkable changes other than my physical achievements would dramatically affect my life.

As a side note many would have thought that injuries resulting from such a careless act as Bobbie Beth's reckless driving would have brought some degree of financial compensation. That was not to be the case. In fact for the second time in my life the opportunity to become a very wealthy young man did not come to pass. As a passenger in an automobile accident I would have been entitled to significant financial remuneration for injuries, medical expenses, loss of projected lifetime earnings, and "pain and suffering." Unfortunately it was discovered through very intensive investigation by my attorney and his private investigator that my legal recourse held little promise for a significant financial settlement. As it turned out the automobile was uninsured and was not technically owned by Bobby. To complicate matters the actual owner indicated he would swear under oath that Bobby did not have permission to drive the car. This information prevented any legal action against the owner for liability in the accident. Any hopes for financial compensation rested solely on a lawsuit against Bobby himself. For three months he dodged being served with notification of the pending lawsuit. Finally he was cornered and forced to accept the court summons. In the end he failed to appear in court, I won the lawsuit, and was officially awarded $2.5 million in settlement. He owned no property and relatively few possessions. In the state of Texas wages cannot be garnished for a civil settlement. Therefore, I am a millionaire on paper only! This failure to obtain rightfully owed financial security for my losses was devastating costing me a couple of thousand dollars in legal fees. It was certainly expensive, physically and financially, and should have been a lesson I learned well. However, so often in life we do not learn from our mistakes.

Over time, as my self-confidence grew with my increased physical independence, old habits reared their ugly heads. It was almost as if I had completely blocked out all of the grief and misery caused by my own selfishness and betrayal. Frequently in our lives we turn our backs on the very people who care most for us. Our overconfidence and arrogance blind us to our own faults and character flaws.

Brandon's work schedule once again shifted after his departure from PRH. He returned to the hectic and time consuming arena of agency nursing typically working the late night shift for better pay. This left me with considerable amounts of time to myself and my wandering ways. Since becoming physically challenged, the nature of our physical relationship had dramatically worsened. It was difficult for Brandon to genuinely share intimacy basically because of the nature of my newly acquired physical challenges. In hindsight I can honestly understand. At the time, I was selfish and lacked any empathy for his feelings in this regard. Naturally, I succumbed to my age old desires and returned to my lecherous bad habits. My drinking, partying, and drug experimentation once again drew me away from home in search of "greener pastures." Considering all that he had tolerated and endured during our relationship my behavior was absolutely shameful!

My gallivanting around town eventually resulted in an affair with a fellow named Robbie that dramatically grew over time. What started out as a one night fling, blossomed into a heated romance of intense physical passion. For several months he and I regularly met at a favorite dance club. I am highly embarrassed to confess that I kept this relationship secret from Brandon who certainly deserved better. Any relationship can only survive when based on mutual trust, honesty, friendship, and love. I allowed myself to be blinded by a fierce yearning for physical pleasure. My selfish desires were further magnified by my renewed use of alcohol and recreational drugs. Use of these party mood enhancers would eventually ruin this relationship as well. Brandon and Robbie were deeply caring individuals who loved me dearly and the loss of both these relationships was my fault and my fault alone. They are but further examples of how devastating and self-destructive alcohol and drugs can be to our lives. My addictive desires for physical pleasure and the deceptive euphoria of mood enhancing elements cost me friendships, at least two relationships, and nearly my life. Unfortunately, it would take several more years of loss and betrayal as well, before I would find my character. Only then was I able to find lasting love and an inner peace.

14 MY NEW LIFE, WHAT A VIEW

TODAY WAS THE day. Moving into Fleetwood Towers was the culmination of personal revelation and physical rehabilitation. The sky was clear, the early morning air a tad crisp for a typical spring day, but this was Texas and "if you don't like the weather, just wait fifteen minutes and it'll change." I must admit this dramatic adventure began with a whirlwind of trepidation and excitement. In the last several years I had completed my essential rehabilitative treatment, wrecked two fine relationships, embarked on a self-destructive experimentation with social "partying and playing" — PAP as it's become known in recent years, and resolved myself to surviving, whatever may come, on my own.

Fleetwood was a quaint "secure" mid-rise tower apartment complex. After weeks of scouring the papers, receiving friendly suggestions, and becoming increasingly discouraged I happened upon the rather notorious residential community tucked quietly away on the outskirts of Oaklawn. For those unfamiliar with this area of Dallas, Texas, suffice it to say that it has acquired the popular reputation of being a "gayborhood." More to the point it was widely regarded as DFW's equivalent to San Francisco. None the less this place was going to suit my initial intentions just fine, or so I thought — that's another story. For now all you need to know is I was living by myself, in my own apartment, without anybody to take care of me. That alone was a gigantic leap; not only of faith, but courage as well.

I had not lived by myself since I graduated from college in 1988, over twelve years before. Furthermore, I had not lived alone since the life altering year of 1992. Either with fraternity brothers, roommates, family, or relationship partners there had always been someone else around. Today was the beginning of a new chapter in my life because now, more than ever, I really needed someone around. Or did I? That was the question I was determined to answer for myself. Within six months my financial recklessness would require the necessity for a roommate regardless of what I wanted.

One's first impression of the "Towers" is ironic. It has only one. As for being secure, well, there were security fences, remote access gates for the parking areas, and supposedly security staff. The individual apartments each had fire and theft detection systems. Each public entryway required a passkey and security card; my idea of safety. As well, the local landmark supposedly had two claims to fame. First, in the early 1960's the infamous nightclub owner Jack Ruby, aka Lee Harvey Oswald's assassin, had once owned and managed a swank private club on the tower's top floor. In addition the Beatles were reportedly to have regularly leased one of the larger apartments during their frequent stays in Dallas. I was never able to document either of these rumors. None the less it made for great small talk.

The leasing staff consisted of a manager, Mick, and his assistant, Jeanette. I was greeted enthusiastically despite my obvious physical challenges. After the passage of the Americans with Disabilities Act (ADA) in 1991, I guess such a response was to be expected. How else should they have reacted? *They were business professionals* offering a product and I was, *seemingly*, a paying customer. Over the years one learns that first impressions can often be misleading no matter what the law may say. Let there be no doubt, these were kind and understanding people who treated me with the greatest of respect and compassion. My only intention is to point out that business is business and reality almost always trumps perception. As long as I met my contractual responsibilities by following the "house rules" and paying the rent, all parties concerned should be happy.

Common sense would normally dictate appropriate measures. However, as has been repeatedly revealed, common sense has not always been my preferred traveling companion. After our initial interview, Jeanette proceeded to show me the available "handicapped accessible" unit on the ground floor. Practical in every way this apartment met any and all requirements for a physically challenged person, with one exception — the view. Only thirty feet from the front office, directly across the hall from the main elevator, this legally appropriate apartment offered a luxurious view of the black tar topped parking lot. Not what I had in mind! This was a tower. I wanted a panoramic vista of my new world, not a 24 hour noisy reminder of my limited capabilities.

Reluctantly I was shown a similar unit on the 2nd floor. I was certain after being informed of the more than twenty-four different floor plans, something else would provide a better scene. Number 235 met with my approval. Now this was more like it! The view was certainly not breathtaking but it was far more appealing than the front end of another resident's car! The slightly more expensive rent was worth it. I was hooked! Certain adjustments would need to be made structurally; every doorway would have to be widened unless I wanted to use the nearest public restroom, an outdoor water hose for a shower, or hang my clothes in plain sight from hooks on the wall. Despite these "adversities", I was assured accommodations could be made within the week. As far as I was concerned, everything was just right. The lease was signed, my initial fees were paid, and I would be in my new home by week's end. Of course any sensible hesitations regarding the need for my evacuation or safety on the 2nd floor in the event of a fire or other emergency were minor. I had a view!

Anyone setting up house for the first time becomes keenly aware immediately that there is more to a home than some pictures, a TV/ stereo, furniture, a few pots and dishes and your clothes. What do you eat? What items are necessary to keep your home clean? How do you fix things without tools? Do vertical blinds really make a room visually appealing? Do you ever outgrow the essential mementos you've treasured from the dormitory days of college life? Needless to say I was far from ready to live by myself for the first time with the realities of my physical limitations. Yet the future held great possibilities as well as challenges. If I could survive what I had lived through before now, then anything was possible. What more could anyone ask for? My new home was "secure," it was a landmark, it was close enough to a wide open world of social possibilities and yet off the beaten path to provide quiet enjoyment, and most importantly it was mine, and mine alone!

The move in brought mixed feelings. As excited as I was to have my own place, relocating required much needed assistance. Despite painful disappointment my last partner graciously and lovingly transported me and all my belongings into #235 Fleetwood Towers. The entire process was conducted efficiently and without disaster. I've learned throughout my life how telling and persuasive eye contact and body language can be. The nature of human interaction is socially and biologically inseparable from the "vibes" we give one another whether intentionally or not. This day was certainly no exception. For the second time in as many years I was awestruck by the mixed feelings permeating the atmosphere around me at the final encounter of someone who supposedly meant so much in my life. In both cases this final departure would be of my own making. Yet this time was significantly different. I had vowed to God and myself that I would never again be dishonest and dishonorable to anyone, especially those I claimed to care about. Those days were over. From this moment forward I was going to live a life of open integrity that I had only hypocritically espoused before. No doubt I had honestly believed my rationalizations until confronted with the vile errors of my own behavior. If nothing else this move to live on my own and by myself would accomplish at least one thing – my mistakes make me a better human being. ADVERSITY would indeed BUILD CHARACTER!

There are quintessential moments in our lives when circumstance causes us to pause and reflect. Self-sufficiency and independent living are two luxuries we often take for granted — *certainly in my case.* After September 28, 1992 the concept of living alone in my own apartment seemed almost as remote as winning the lottery. Yet, nearly 8 years later I had achieved that remarkable milestone. This accomplishment was solely the result of lessons learned from years of strife and turmoil. My life had been a far cry from those who have survived starvation, social upheaval, or natural disaster. However, my life struggles had been numerous and troubling. As well, my short thirty-five year lifespan had seen miraculous character transitions that can only be described as the cornerstones of a life well lived. As the years have passed and I've grown *older and wiser* the errors of my ways have served me well to be more grateful, more gracious, more charitable and certainly less gullible. Only time will tell if my experiences will be equally beneficial to help others cope with the slings and arrows life throws their way.

Life Is ... Accept It Or Change It

ADVERSITY *DOES* BUILD Character. A few times in my life, as I am sure in every human life, there have been monumental events to transcend all previous experiences and alter my thinking forever. For some it might be a photo. For others it could be a word or phrase. Then again it could be a chance encounter with someone or even a single shared moment in the same classroom of life. Whatever the experience, we remember them for the rest of our lives. I was once told that these are known as "breakthroughs". I began this book with a quote from Scripture, and throughout my tale I have repeatedly referred to and acknowledged my gratefulness to God, among others. This quote was one such breakthrough for me, for it demonstrated thanksgiving for the blessings one had received. One friend advised that I should tone down my "religious" references to increase the potential readership, because we live in an ever growing secular world of "non-believers;" *Perhaps.*

Though I may be a Christian, I am also philosophical. The French philosopher, Voltaire, once wrote, "I may not believe that you are right, but I will defend your right to say it to the death." Ironically enough, he also wrote, "God is a comedian, whose audience is afraid to laugh!" Obviously his philosophy did not impede his sense of humor. Whatever your belief system allows you or disallows you to accept as far as a supreme being, I hope that you will bear with me just a little longer, for I hope to challenge all readers to a higher purpose — having gratitude or thanksgiving. *No matter how bad your adversity, take a look around, and you'll find someone who has it worse. So be grateful for what you have and realize it can __always__ be worse.*

Life never ceases to surprise me, for I am always filled with respect that my life has not been that bad. Once I was in one of my favorite hangouts with an acquaintance. The barkeep served my beverage and I tipped him a fair tip. He acknowledged my generosity with a hearty thank you. I replied, "The good Lord has been good to me why can't I be good to others." My friend peered down at me in my wheelchair shaking his head. I inquired why. He explained that he knew hundreds if not thousands of people, who if faced with what I had been through could not possibly have responded with such a positive outlook on life. I spoke from the heart with the first thought that came to mind. I noted that I had people who loved me, a roof over my head, food in my gut, clothes on my back, and a job to support me. As a recently popular song so perfectly phrased it, "I could not ask for more!" There are so many in this world not so fortunate.

The 80's "me generation" philosophy has so dulled our sense of duty and generosity that we have forgotten how truly good we have it in this country. I remember Grandma Bolte explaining to me why she saved tinfoil and old pantyhose. It was a Great Depression habit that had left a lasting impression upon her. In one brief moment it was made very clear that my lifetime had seen great luxury in comparison to hers. Those hard times had made her a formidable woman of strength, and taught her to improvise in a rationed world. As an avid student of history and international relations I have been truly blessed with a small sense of wisdom about the world around me, at home and abroad. It was once said that one could never understand the life of a fisherman *without first walking in his shoes*. I am also reminded that this fact, in and of itself, *cannot begin to compare to the life of a man who has no feet*.

At every turn I have been humbled by the fact that no matter how massive and ugly my problems may have seemed, every one of us has trials and tribulations. Yours may appear trite and of little consequence to me and vice versa, but in all they are part of life, good and bad. When driving through the city streets are we not humbled somewhat by the homeless on the curb, even if we may think that they are just panhandlers. Many living in Maytag boxes are not. How can we feel smug with thousands of children dying from hunger and disease? Adversity *should* Build Charity. Even the rich and privileged have adversity, though it may seem trivial to the rest of us. Though they may not have to worry about hunger or homelessness, their families have dysfunction and pain just like so many others. Wealth does not lead to happiness or even comfort for many. I have been fortunate to see "how the other half lives" by association, and I know that they experience the human condition also — only in nicer surroundings. This begs the question "why can't we help our fellow man?" I'm living proof that your life can be completely changed in a split second. Am I less of a human being because of it? Do I have fewer rights, or for that matter any more rights because of my adversity? On the contrary, because of that life altering experience, I am a more sensitive human being and entitled to the same as anyone. I am the same man I have always been; only now I am truly sorry for lying to myself for so many years. With age comes wisdom and the only difference now is that my fervor has been tempered by experience. However, I ask not for pity just the right to live life to my fullest potential. Isn't that what each of us really wants? Why do we not offer and expect the same from everyone else?

Many would say that this altruistic notion is naïve and contrary to the world we live in. I say, "Bullshit!" Have we become so materialistic that we can no longer expect the best in each of us? What happened to "Camelot"? Our children are trying to tell us something — "from the mouths of babes." With children selling and using drugs, shooting each other in their schools, and the talk shows giving endless examples of violent and abusive children, can we not hear the music? Love and direction at home are the foundations of good citizens and decent human beings. All the money in the world and endless government programs will not end the debacle of our forgotten future. Every generation will blame the one before for the woes they must endure, as they have done for millennia. That should not impede our endeavor to become better human beings. To come full circle, my adversity cannot be blamed on the rest of the world, for the rest of the world has adversity too. My challenge is simply this; accept your hardships and deal with them — that's life. Make our world a better place and our race a little nobler by doing your part to be more charitable and accepting. During the French Revolution, a phrase was coined that fits —"Nobles 'Oblige." Basically because of the good in your life, whatever it may be, you have an obligation to spread it around. Your good fortune obligates you to be charitable, and in many ways, demonstrates your gratitude for the blessings you have received. Alternately, the pain in your life is no excuse for forgetting that fact – we all have pain! Get over it!

In the aforementioned quote from Scripture, the Samaritan gave praise to God and thanked Jesus for his healing. Christ noted "your faith has made you well." In a more contemporary slant, we note that it is far better to give than receive. In this country we have declared a national holiday of Thanksgiving. Once a year, at Christmas we treat all human beings as brothers and sisters. What if we live every day like Thanksgiving and Christmas? I'm not advocating the commercialized holidays necessarily, but rather the spirit of the season for the good of all humankind. Am I dreamer? Perhaps, but even the simplest of breakthroughs began as dreams. Without dreams man is but another carbon based life form on this cosmic dust speck we call Earth.

For me *Adversity Builds Character* is my small way of trying to help others as others have helped me. There is no magic formula to life; for life is constantly changing. Only by understanding that life is constantly changing can we begin to deal with life itself. As babies we are absorbing and dealing with endless changing environment and conditions. As adults the only thing that is different is our reluctance to accept change and our staunch comfort with stagnation — a façade in itself. Life is an endless barrage of change. If Darwin taught us anything it is that to survive we must deal with change and adapt to it. Adversity is life's way of making us stronger. Ask this question: which is easier, walking or learning to live without walking? If our species began its lifecycle slithering through the world, would it not then be more difficult to learn to get up and walk? Does this not possibly explain why it took Homo sapiens millions of years to become Homo erectus? For so many of us, cherished notions and dogmas are the most difficult to maintain and uphold when confronted by true adversity. Our perspectives change when hunger, poverty, sickness and/or other adversities aren't merely knocking at the door, but unashamedly sitting at the dinner table gorging down the last crumbs of our hope. For that matter, when adversity is standing calmly by with a smirk of satisfaction at the nearby graves of those we've loved how will you respond? *Life is as life is — either accept it, change it, or let it kill you*, but constantly bitching and complaining doesn't help anyone, least of all you!

THE END

TOM UFERT

"Adversity Is A Splendid Thing"

WHAT'S WRONG WITH ADVERSITY?
IT PROVES WE'RE ALIVE.
IF THERE WAS NO ADVERSITY
LIFE WOULD BE ONLY A FANTASY
AND NO FANTASY EVER LASTS...
BUT LIFE CAN. IT IS ETERNAL.
ALL OF OUR MEMORIES,
GOOD AND BAD,
ARE OURS AND THEY PROLONG LIFE.
ALL THE COLORS OF LIFE,
BRIGHT AND DARK,
ARE THE RAINBOWS OF US ALL —
THEY MAKE UP THE GLORIOUS TAPESTRY
OF ALL HUMANITY.
WITHOUT A SINGLE ONE, NO MATTER HOW
THIN OR DEMUR,
THE MAJESTIC PAINTING WOULD BE INCOMPLETE
AND FULL OF HOLES.
NEVER GIVE UP.
FALL BACK...RETREAT & REGROUP...TAKE A BREAK,
BUT NEVER GIVE UP!
LIVE LIFE IN ALL OF ITS JOYS AND PAINS,
FOR EACH AND EVERY MOMENT
IS A SPLENDID THING.

Tom Ufert, 2004

Author's Note

Scripture quotations in this work came from my family Bible, The Holy Bible, New Catholic version by P.J. Kennedy and Sons. Additional quotations were taken from the Dictionary of Quotations edited by Bergen Evans.

I wish to offer my deepest thanks to my dear friend Joan Falkowski for literally hours of advice and suggestions regarding every manner of design, format, and the contractual details necessary to properly select a designer.

Words cannot express my deepest thanks for the generosity and creativity of Ron Comstock. An accomplished photographer, he thoughtfully conceived and produced each of the author photos that accompany this book. In addition Ron's talented skills were responsible for the creation of my book cover, author's logo, and website. A large portion of his hard work was donated free of charge out of friendship and a genuine desire to assist in the completion of my work. Furthermore, I wish to acknowledge sincere gratitude to the staff and management of Sam's Furniture & Appliance, Inc. in Haltom City, Texas, for their gracious assistance in supplying an exquisite setting for some of the photography shoots.

Significant praise and appreciation must also be given to a select group of people who generously agreed to proof read and constructively critique my writing and style before submitting the book for publication. These individuals include my former high school English teacher Sharon D.

Smith, my dear friends Joan Falkowski, Lester W. Van Huss, Michelle Spann, and Randy McBrayer. Each of these individuals offered their own unique perspective that significantly contributed to over a decade's worth of work. A further note of deeply felt gratitude must be expressed to WriteIntoPrint, member of the Alliance of Independent Authors, for their gracious assistance and outstanding expertise in the initial transposing of this work to ebook form. In addition I would be remiss if extensive credit were not given to the outstanding staff at IUniverse Publishing for their patient and creative efforts to help my dream of becoming a published author become a reality.

Finally, it must be noted that *Adversity Builds Character; An Inspirational True Life Story of Disability, Addiction and Acceptance* would have never been possible had it not been for the inspiration and persistence of my godmother/grandmother Joy V. Campbell. For years prior to her passing in 2008 she constantly stressed that my life experience was a story that needed to be told in the hope of helping others deal with life's adversities. I thank God for her insistence in this endeavor and know deep in my heart that her guiding spirit helped bring this book to fruition.

Author's Biography

Tom Ufert, a 46 year old quadriplegic afflicted with three different disabilities is an inspirational voice in our troubled times. He received his bachelor of arts in political science and history as a scholarship recipient from Centenary College of Louisiana. Tom is a former Rotary International graduate Fellow who attended Australian National University in Canberra, ACT, specializing in East Asian political affairs and was a White House Fellow nominee. He is a former Lyndon Baines Johnson congressional intern and constituency aid for two former United States members of Congress. His past services for 11 political campaigns on both sides of the aisle were highly valued by former Governor of Louisiana, Charles "Buddy" Roemer, United States Vice President George W. H. Bush's former assistant chief of staff Henson W. Moore, and the present U.S. Trade Ambassador, the Honorable Ron Kirk.

At age 23 he was the youngest artistic Board Chairman in the United States as head of the Shreveport Summer Music Festival. Mr. Ufert has served as a member of two other 501(c) three charity boards including his beloved fraternity Phi Mu Alpha Sinfonia as well as the community advisory board for his former rehabilitation hospital. His professional memberships include Phi Alpha Theta, Sigma Tau Delta, and the Worldwide Who's Who. In recent years he has worked tirelessly as a volunteer fundraiser for numerous AIDS charities in his community and served briefly as the community affairs liaison for Legacy Founders Cottage. Tom Ufert, a native of Louisiana, now resides in Texas.